SPIRITUAL
HUNGER

Integrating Myth and Ritual into Daily Life

Other books by **Allan G. Hunter**

The Path of Synchronicity
Princes, Frogs & Ugly Sisters
Stories We Need to Know
The Six Archetypes of Love
Write Your Memoir
The Sanity Manual
From Coastal Command to Captivity

SPIRITUAL HUNGER

Integrating Myth and Ritual into Daily Life

Dr. Allan G. Hunter

FINDHORN PRESS

© Allan G. Hunter 2012

The right of Allan G. Hunter to be identified as the author
of this work has been asserted by him in accordance
with the Copyright, Designs and Patents Act 1998.

Published in 2012 by Findhorn Press, Scotland

ISBN 978-1-84409-560-5

A CIP record for this title is available from the British Library.

Edited by Nicky Leach
Cover design by Richard Crookes
Interior design by Damian Keenan
Printed and bound in the USA

1 2 3 4 5 6 7 8 9 18 17 16 15 14 13 12

Published by

Findhorn Press

117-121 High Street,

Forres IV36 1AB,

Scotland, UK

t +44 (0)1309 690582

f +44 (0)131 777 2711

e info@findhornpress.com

www.findhornpress.com

CONTENTS

Acknowledgments 9

PART I
Spiritual Hunger: What It Is, How It Works, And Why We Need Myths

1 Ritual as a Way of Making Meaning 12
2 The Nature of Spiritual Hunger 14
3 Rituals and Myths That Have Lost Their Power 22
4 So What Do We Do? One Size Does Not Fit All 27

PART II
The Advantages Of Ritual: Learning To Listen To Your Heart

5 The Nature of Ritual and Myth 33
6 Myth Doesn't Have to Be True to Reveal Truth 40
7 How Ritual Can Put Us In Touch With the Present 46

PART III
How To See Beneath The Surface: Some Practical Examples Of Rituals And Myths In Action

8 The Mythic Landscape:
      The World Is Our Sacred Dwelling Place 50
9 The Palio di Siena:
      A Ritual of Social Competition 59
10 Dangerous Myths:
      Gun Ownership and War 62
11 Ritual Occasions That Have Changed Their Emphasis:
      Childbirth 71
12 Myth Is Everywhere — If You Look For It 75

PART IV
We Need Myths,
But How Can We Choose Productive Myths?
Some Practical Guidelines

13 Bogus Myths and How To Identify Them 80

14 What Do Myth and Ritual Supply? 84

15 Some Devalued Rituals:
Jury Duty, The Drinking Age 90

16 A Ritual We All Think We Know:
Graduation 96

17 A Ritual That Has Endured:
Marriage 99

18 The Role of the Unconscious in Ritual Actions -
The Mute Message of Funerals 102

PART V
The Cost Of Not Embracing The Mythic Aspects Of Life

19 What We Can Expect in a World of Weak Myths 110

20 A World Without Coherent Rituals and Myths:
Boredom 118

CONTENTS

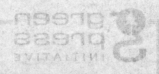

PART VI

Everyday Myth: Finding Soul Sustenance
To Get You Through Each Day

21 Work:
   Burden or Ritual Opportunity? 122

22 What Sorts of Myths Do We Need? 126

23 Rituals of Food:
   Dietary Norms and Strictures 132

24 Underappreciated Rituals – Cars, and Kitchens:
   Establishing Our Ritual Space 135

25 A Theory of Ritual and Myth:
   Choosing the Way Forward 143

26 Ritual is the Activity That Makes Us Human:
   A Primary Structure of the Psyche 150

PART VII

Conclusion

27 What it all Means:
   Myth and Ritual and the Six Archetypes 154

Notes 165

Bibliography 170

Acknowledgments

This book has been the result of many years of thinking about ritual and myth, and so thanking those involved may seem all but impossible. Nevertheless, I will try.

First and foremost, I wish to thank those who allowed me the time and space to explore these ideas in writing. The President of Curry College, Ken Quigley, and the members of the board of trustees generously allowed me release time for the completion of the text. Particularly helpful along the way were my colleagues Dean Susan Pennini, Dr. Tom Byrne, Dr. Gabrielle Regney, and Dr. Kara Provost; Professors Jeannette De Jong, Jeffrey DiIuglio, and Marcy Holbrook were valued supporters throughout.

I wish also to thank the trustees of the Seth Sprague Educational and Charitable Foundation, specifically Mrs. Arline Greenleaf and Mrs. Rebecca Greenleaf-Clapp, for their continuing support of the Honors Program at Curry College. Many of the ideas that appear in these pages were first explored within that program, and I am grateful every day for their support of it and its aims. Dr. Ronald Warners, as Director of the Program, deserves special mention for his ongoing support of my research.

Those who helped me in other ways include Suzanne Strempek Shea, who seems to be able to spread inspiration effortlessly wherever she goes; David Whitley (Cambridge University) who gave me gentle guidance on so many issues; Laura Warrell, who challenged and questioned so helpfully; and Cat Bennett, who put so many excellent ideas forward—and always does. Dr Jack Kahn was especially encouraging; some of the ideas in this book were first presented as a paper at the 19th annual Personal Construct Psychology Conference, of which he was co-chair.

Baptist De Pape deserves a particular mention, as does Mattijs van Moorsel. Conversations with them are always a delight and that never fail to provoke further thoughts in me. My gratitude is immense that they are part of my life and world.

Brittany Capozzi, Nora Klaver, Douglas Kornfeld, Cathrine Lodoen, Lilou Mace, Paula Ogier, Maggie Stern, Kat Tansey, Justine and Michael Toms at New Dimensions Media, and Sally Young were also an important part of this process, and I owe them gratitude, one and all.

Particularly deserving of thanks are Thierry Bogliolo, the finest publisher anyone could ask for, and many thanks also to Nicky Leach, who is both a delightful editor and a contributor of outstanding insights. Cynthia Barralis, Richard Crookes, Damian Keenan, Carol Shaw, Gail Torr, and Sabine Weeke also contributed far more than they may realize. I am deeply grateful to you all.

NOTE: In these pages I frequently refer to things my workshop participants and students have shared in open class discussions. I have concealed the identities of these people out of respect for their privacy, while staying true to the nature of the experiences they describe. I am grateful to you all for your openness. The examples taken from my own life are, of course, true.

PART I

Spiritual Hunger:
What It Is, How It Works,
And Why We Need Myths

CHAPTER ONE

Ritual as a Way of Making Meaning

This is a true story. A bored 11-year old boy walks across the stage as he graduates from sixth grade, his parents looking on. Later that night, he is taken on a drive into gang territory and given a shotgun, which he then fires eight times at short range into a group of rival gang members. Returning home, he feels proud that his initiation into his local gang has gone so well. [1]

It's a chilling example, but it makes the point. What happens if we lose sight of the safe, socially sanctioned rituals of our culture? We are ritual-creating creatures, since ritual helps us to hold onto and emphasize meaning. Most of us don't choose such violent or dramatic ways of doing things as this gang member. But we do like our habits and our routines.

And what are these except forms of ritual?

We continually make meanings whenever we form a judgment as to whether something is good or bad—and we do that all the time—but we may not always do it in the most effective or humane ways. That young gang member, "Monster" Kody Scott—with his reverence for the gang's signifiers, codes, and precise sense of form—was opting for a specific ritualized way of life, one that he felt gave him status and value. In other words, he was trying to find meaning in a world that to him was meaningless.

He was far from alone in his response. On the other side of the equation, the teenage girl who gets pregnant in order to feel grown up is, in many cases, doing the exact same thing. Once she has a child, she has a meaning and a purpose she might not feel she had ever had before. It would be easy to multiply examples.

What is important here is to notice that these actions of killing or getting pregnant are premeditated, and to a great extent consciously chosen. We cannot ignore them or consider them simply as confused mistakes. They are part of a ritual way of thinking, a need that runs deep in all humanity. If we try to dismiss these behaviors by calling them psychopathic, then how do we explain the huge numbers of young people who are eager to follow this path? Surely, they can't all be psychopaths.

If this example feels remote from us, I'd point instead to the pervasive tendency in the United States for ordinary citizens to create mythic meanings.

Consider the Revolutionary War of 1776. It was all about getting rid of the British monarchy and its aristocratic power structures; yet what we see is that we have spontaneously re-created a monarchy of sorts at a popular level, using celebrities. So we may not have kings any more, but we have "the artist formerly known as Prince." We have "Duke" Ellington, "The Duke" John Wayne, "The King" Elvis, "Count" Basie, "Lady" Gaga, and Madonna, who threatens to replace the Queen of Heaven in popularity. President John F. Kennedy's White House became in the public imagination "Camelot"—a clear reference to King Arthur's mythic palace in Britain. In addition, we have a tendency to turn our media stars into rulers—Arnold Schwarzenegger and Ronald Reagan are just two high-profile examples, while the movie star Grace Kelly married and became Princess Grace of Monaco. We may have banished the monarchy, but something in us causes us to re-create it in another form. We seem to yearn for the mythic and the ritual.

The question that arises is not whether rituals are good or bad; more precisely, it's whether we will choose rituals that are productive or unproductive—because we're going to have rituals, one way or another. In fact, whenever we look at our society and see an area of crisis, a place where we have a "social problem," there's a fair chance we'll find we're looking at a situation where the old, safe rituals that "held" the meaning of a significant event have been erased or supplanted by something else.

As one man I worked with said to me: "Every kid I knew on my street had done time in jail. So I had to do something, too, to show I wasn't a wimp. What did I do? I robbed a liquor store and got sent to jail."

As a society, we can respond to this sort of reaction by building more jails. We can hire more police. We can get more social workers involved. Unfortunately, these responses will not cure the underlying malaise, which in the examples of the young offenders we've looked at has to do specifically with the loss of significant rituals: those that mark the transition to adulthood.

When social rituals fail, people create personal rituals, some of which are destructive. In every instance the underlying problem has to do with a desire to live in a world that feels significant—in other words, it's a case of spiritual hunger.

CHAPTER TWO

The Nature of Spiritual Hunger

These days, spiritual hunger is mostly seen only in its negative aspect. Most people experience it as that feeling that nothing much matters, that we don't care much about anything or anyone, not even ourselves. We may feel it as a lack of love, a lack of meaning that seeps into our lives.

Unfortunately, a growing body of people all over the world report feeling this same emptiness. Depression, for example, has often been linked to this sense of lack of meaning. Approximately one in four Americans will suffer from depression at some time in their lives—and those are just the people who report it. Compulsive activities and addictions can blunt this feeling, at least for a while. They give a direction to a life that has no direction, but at a dreadful cost.

In this book I'm going to show you how you can push back against this tide of despair and find deep meaning in your life. This is because spiritual hunger is, in itself, entirely natural. We long for meaningful connection to something bigger than ourselves. We yearn to know that we are not alone in our situation in life, and that others have been in similar situations and survived. When we find this knowledge we can feel more centered in our lives, our culture, our world. This is the positive side of spiritual hunger. It urges us to find more meaning in our world. It asks us to look more deeply into the experience of being alive.

So where can we find this sense of connection? The answer may surprise us. We can learn how to feed our own souls if we pay attention to literature, to myth, and to another form of "story": ritual.

Words like "ritual" are treated with suspicion these days, and the idea itself has become tarnished. It has the smell of old churches, dust, and candle smoke about it. And, in fact, we've abandoned many of the venerated rites and formalities our ancestors would have upheld energetically. Often this is a great relief, but when we throw out a ritual, what is it we're throwing out, exactly? In many cases we're rejecting the understandings and reassurances that held earlier generations together, the actions that provided them with a sense of social stability.

Researcher Brene Brown put it well when she said, "Stories are data with soul," and we can extend this and say that ritual actions are a way of creating a lasting story, where the information takes on permanent value, and so gives us a way to remember it.[1] In the process it can open our hearts to the deep significance of the occasion—but only if we choose a productive and nurturing ritual.

On the whole, we live today in a culture that is strangely devoid of meaningful customs, and where ritual has been stripped of its sense of story. For example, children progress through our schools in a sort of lock-step that has to do with exams and graduating. Unfortunately, the emphasis is on the exams and passing them rather than on developing a sense of personal awareness or individual responsibility that might be a better way of approaching adulthood. Certainly that would be more helpful in navigating the outside world. Any deeply felt rituals of "graduation" and of being promoted to new levels of personal competence have been ignored. For many people high-school graduation itself has been reduced to an excuse to dress up, and little more. The heart's need for an affirmation that real change has occurred is left untended.

Here's another example. Almost everyone takes a driving test. It's just a chore we have to get through. Yet huge numbers of teenage drivers in the United States kill themselves and others because they can't handle the responsibility of being in charge of a large, powerful motor vehicle. It's the leading cause of death for American teens.[2]

This is something we really ought to be concerned about, yet even a quick look at the situation will show us that these young people have been trained for the test but not taught about how to handle their own responses to power. Is this really so very far removed from the ancient legend of the young Phaeton, who begged his father Helios to let him drive the sun-chariot, lost control of it, and was killed? The Greeks had that legend for a reason.

Again, in the United States, we have the right to "bear arms." As a result, every year about 12,000 people die in gun-related incidents. That's a lot of coffins. It's close to three times as many deaths as were incurred by US forces in nearly 10 years of full-scale war in Iraq.

My point is that the law guarantees these rights, but there are few understandings about the *responsibilities* involved. Laws cannot save us from ourselves; responsibilities can. And these responsibilities are traditionally taught through story, legend, and ritual. Laws are always about lower, external compulsions to conform, while responsibilities require us to use our higher moral awareness and involve our hearts more fully in the business of living. Yet we cannot live from this higher heart-awareness if we're only looking at getting what we can get right now in order to keep up with our peers. This sense of competition, of ego gratification, actually separates us from everyone else. In contrast, a responsibility makes us more aware of our connection to our community, and this is a heart-based connection.

Without this heart-based connection many people tend to feel lost, so they act in ways that are not always healthy. This is especially dangerous for our young people. Religion no longer seems sufficiently strong to uphold the cultural values we once lived by, and anyway, our culture is changing too fast for most of us to comprehend. That's why so many of us suffer from spiritual hunger. We know we need something to nourish our sense of being, our sense of purpose, and of belonging, but we can't find much that will satisfy that need.

If we accept that we can look for guidance to those long-neglected myths, legends, and rituals that exist in our culture, we'll need to see how they work so that we can feed our hearts and spirits. For all three of these sources of guidance depend upon us knowing the stories or ritual actions so that we can practice vital life lessons and become aware of our limits before a crisis arises.

Let me give you an example.

I once asked students at one of my writing workshops to define courage. Courage is a word that derives from the French word *coeur*, meaning "heart," so *coeur-age* has an underlying meaning of living from the heart.

The workshop members considered this and other ideas, and we had a lively and far-ranging discussion but, in the end, we all agreed on a definition: Courage is, in large part, knowing the right thing to do, then doing it—no matter how frightened you may be. So the "right thing to do" is based in a knowing that exists not in the mind but in the heart.

It's a pretty good definition. As it happens it also applies to military training, where recruits are taught how to manage their fear and stick to their guns so that they will continue to do what they're told, no matter what. Some people call that brainwashing, but I'm not so sure we can always jump to that conclusion. Doing the right thing while under stress depends upon repressing the desire to run away, so courage is at some level always about being prepared for what happens.

Being prepared gives us better options. We don't panic. We make better decisions because we're acting rather than reacting. It happens because we are telling ourselves a new story about who we are. When we do this we are no longer ruled by blind impulses. What this means is that courage is, to a large extent, about being sufficiently aware so that we can move through fear to a place of making strong choices—reasoned choices—when others might succumb to panic.

On the whole, good decisions come when we are in a calm and centered place, and bad decisions happen when we're agitated, angry, or frightened. Courage and wisdom are, therefore, inextricably linked. In contrast, panic is always about me, about saving my skin. Courage and wisdom are always about community, and these are loving energies, since they do not see us as separate from one another. The wise decision helps everyone, not just the decider.

This is also a first-class recipe for getting through life. If I'm prepared for the likelihood that an acquaintance or relative is going to say something cruel, then I am not forced into being defensive and don't have to feel hurt. I can choose to act from compassion, instead. More simply, if I know what a skid is, when my car skids on snow and ice I will know what to do to get safely through the situation without endangering myself or others. Wisdom is not just about knowing the right thing to do; it's being able to keep on knowing it even when under stress.

Our mental health depends largely on understanding this. When a toddler screams at us we don't have to take it personally, because it's just a toddler screaming at us. That is a healthy reaction. Yet some people hit their children because they don't know there's any other way to react.

So we can see that training ourselves for whatever delights and disasters happen in our lives is—within reason—an entirely sensible way forward. It means that life experiences are no longer quite as raw and surprising as they might otherwise be. They can be understood through talking about the experience, sharing the knowledge— and that is also a ritual action.

Cultures depend upon this offering of vital advice in the form of stories and literature for exactly the same reason: to prepare us for whatever human situations will come and give us a standard of conduct that we can compare ourselves to. And they've done so for thousands of years. Some of that wisdom and awareness has been codified in rituals and myths. We can survive without this information, of course, but our lives will be qualitatively different. Ritual, at its core, creates a sense of order in what might otherwise seem like a chaotic world.

But there is more. When we feel connected to a meaningful ritual what we feel is gratitude for the wisdom in it, and that sense of gratitude is felt not in the mind but in the heart. Meaningful ritual—ritual that we understand thoroughly—is a way to open the heart and keep us in a place of real gratitude for the wonders of our life. It feeds our spiritual hunger and brings us closer to one another; the lack of it feels like loneliness and desolation.

Let me tell you a story that illustrates this.

When I was 10 years old, my parents decided to send me to a good, old-fashioned British boarding school—a "public school" with ivy on the walls and headmasters with canes with which some of us were routinely thrashed.

From a practical point of view, the decision to send me away was actually a good one: I had a scholarship, so my education would cost very little. My brother had gone to a similar school before this. It would help me grow up. It was socially acceptable to treat small boys this way. By many of the standards of the day, it was the "correct" thing to do. At the age of 10, though, none of this made any sense to me. All I could think was, "How could you do this to me?" I'd worked hard, been a good boy, done my homework, got the scholarship—and now they were abandoning me to this hellhole!

I knew how grim and spartan such places could be because my brother had also shed bitter tears when he was sent away, and told sad tales of loneliness, cruelty, theft, and bullying, on his return. Or perhaps I should say that he told us very little about these things, but we could feel them, even so. The stiff upper lip didn't conceal the pain. We were both tall for our age, but there were mean older kids who were tall for their ages, too, and who vented their own sense of abandonment on the new kids. "Lambs to the slaughter" is a phrase that springs all too readily to mind.

I attended that school for seven years. I *did* get an excellent education, as it happened, but I also learned to trust no one. My mind was highly educated—but not my heart, nor my spirit.

Decades later I read about initiation rites in various non-Western societies, especially Papuan and Australian aboriginal rituals, which were broadly speaking an echo of many other rites across the globe. In those societies, the pubertal male child is taken away from the mother and the women's compound where, until now, he has been a rather pampered little lord.[3]

In an elaborate pantomime that the adults know only too well, the boy is snatched away by the male members of the tribe, who are dressed in ferocious ways, making terrifying noises, perhaps wearing masks so they are not identifiable, and behaving quite unlike their usual selves. The women wail as if they fear the boys will be killed.

The scared young boys are then taken to the designated ritual place and are given ritual scars. In some cultures they may be circumcised, and they generally undergo brief but painful rites. At the end of this they are made to realize that they are part of the men's compound now. They cannot go back to their mothers in the same way as before. They are told they are the latest recruits to the male society and that everything will change, now. The older men then congratulate them on their bravery and endurance, and welcome them lovingly into a new way of life, explaining that this is for their own good.

If we think about it for a moment this ritual has a certain eloquence. It tells the young boy that his relationship to women and to his mother will change, that it *must* change, and from now on he has certain responsibilities he has to fulfill. The ritual and the scars impress this on his mind and his body.

You can imagine the situation. After the boy has recovered from his shock, and after he's grown a little older and been part of helping other younger boys through the same rituals, he'll see the deep significance of what must have at first seemed to be meaningless cruelty. He'll see that he has a place in the world, a right to be a male that has nothing to do with whether he gets a good job or joins the country club. It makes him part of a living myth about who he is.

At the age of 10, I went through something very similar in its general outline. The difference was that no one knew it was a ritual, so no one knew it had any psychic significance. It was just an unpleasant fact. Together with the other boys, I thought we'd all been delivered into a life of misery and unpleasantness. We felt that this was desperately unjust, so we became bitter, resentful, and callous to each other at the very moment when we could have used some loving support. Our world felt like a cruel place, and because it felt like that, that is exactly what we made it into.

Lacking any sense of the new form our lives had taken, or its significance, we fell back into the only form that was available to us: We bullied and victimized each other. This was a ritual of sorts, too—one that we created for ourselves. In schools and colleges in the United States today, this is still a problem. Whether we call it cyber-bullying, which has caused teenagers to commit suicide (several such cases are under discussion in the media today, in 2011), or whether it's just written off as "hazing," it's basically the same brutality.

If, as schoolboys, we had known that there was a deep echo of an ancient and meaningful ritual in our experiences, if this information had ever been made available to us, then I'm sure we could all have learned to see our life situation in a different way. It wouldn't have been a case of "my life feels like hell" but, rather, a sense that this was a test that would humanize us.

Unfortunately, we only got the first part of the meaning and totally missed the second. If we'd known the overall outline of what was going on it would have helped us to cultivate our awareness, and with it our courage, and perhaps many other qualities, including trust, and a sense of the dignity of human existence. Life would have had a shape we could have identified, and it would have been less random, chaotic, and frightening.

Whatever it was we learned at that time, it was certainly not courage. I can see that now. I had lived through a pubertal ritual without knowing what it was. And if you don't know what a thing is, it's very hard to see meaning in it.

The point I wish to make is this: If we—that crowd of little boys—had been able to see what was going on shortly after the event, then we'd have made more sense of it. We'd have been able to live our lives with greater courage, knowing that we had to mobilize our own best selves from now on.

But we didn't. During our vacations, we went home and were overly cosseted by our guilt-ridden mothers and indulged by our bewildered fathers. Then, at the start of each new semester, we were sent out into the wilderness again. The shock of this change was like having an old wound reopened, each time a little deeper. We hadn't broken free of our mothers at all, it seemed, and we certainly weren't the equals of our fathers. So where were we? Frightened, for one thing, and desperate not to show it.

An opportunity for psychic growth and for meaningful mutual support had been squandered. The authentic spiritual development of thousands of boys like me had stalled, and for some would never restart.

The experience wasn't all bad—many of us learned self-sufficiency, and real, vital friendships did grow amid the ruins—but it could have been so much more.

What we'll discover as we move through these pages is that many useful myths and rituals have been discarded and neglected in today's "rational" world, which has no time for such thoughts. The cost has frequently been that with nothing much to replace these beliefs, young people have felt themselves to be adrift, even lost.

In contrast, we'll see that the creation of myth and ritual is as natural and vital to humans as eating. As with eating, though, we need guidance or we'll gorge ourselves on candy and rot our teeth. Many of the myths of the present day are like candy: easy to consume and not good for us. Other myths seem to be missing entirely. In this book, I'll be surveying some current myths, some of which are candy-like and ultimately destructive. Then I will show you how to choose your own myths, so you can nourish your psyche successfully for the rest of your life.

Our most vital link is, after all, to eternity. It is to the majesty of the stars in the heavens, the beauty of the earth, and the awareness that we are all interconnected. The shiny toys placed before us by those who want us to follow the ego path of separateness will not connect us to anything except gnawing discontent. We have only ritual and myth to remind us of this, to tell us that others have been this way before us. Only ritual and myth can bring us back to the heart space of knowing we are all connected, and help us to make meaningful lives. It may, in fact, be true to say that it is an awareness of ritual and myth that makes us fully human, since without these attributes in our lives we tend to feel lost.

Perhaps Edward Gibbon described this situation best, with all its challenges, writing in 1837 in *The History of the Decline and Fall of The Roman Empire*:

So urgent on the vulgar [the ordinary citizens] is the necessity
of believing, that the fall of any system of mythology will most
probably be succeeded by the introduction of some other mode
of superstition.[4]

This seems to be exactly our situation today, as we have shed our reverence for the
older mythic structures of our world, and replaced them with something provided by
marketing companies.

Overview

So let's spell this out: The desire to find meaning in our lives is primal, and it can
lead in two different directions. It can lead toward understanding and deep, loving
connection, where our spiritual hunger is satisfied, or it can lead toward compulsive
actions, extremist beliefs, and destructive behaviors that feed the ego. Unfortunately,
our society is at present much more consistent in choosing the negative path. We
don't have to follow that route.

In the chapters that follow we'll identify the belief structures that can nourish our
souls, and reject those that don't. Much of the guidance we need is embedded in the
myths, rituals, and beliefs we already have, if we take the time to understand them.
The trouble is that we have lost sight of their true meanings, and we now need to
reclaim them so that we can integrate them into our lives.

If the world is to move toward peace and harmony we'll have to achieve personal
peace, as well as that sense of connectedness to the eternal that we can only access
through understanding productive rituals and myths. As we look at these rituals and
myths, what we'll discover is that they are a way to articulate who we think we are.
As such, they are closely linked to the kind of awareness that makes us distinctively
human, and far more than just highly intelligent mammals.

At the end of the book, I will show you that all life-giving rituals and myths are
connected to one of the primary, deep structures of the psyche, since they are the
surface manifestations of an ancient and pervasive wisdom that we have neglected.
This wisdom has to do with the stages of development we can expect to go through as
we move to full personal empowerment. It exists as a string of connected archetypes
that illustrate the growth points we can expect to face. The rituals, the myths, and the
stories are the surface manifestations of this deeper structure.

Rituals and Myths That
Have Lost Their Power

Recalling the plight of the young boys in my public school, discussed in the previous chapter, we might ask: What can we do about rituals that have lost their
power and myths that fail to capture the imagination?

For one thing, I'm reluctant to propose that we start implementing various odd
rites and ceremonies, or that we borrow religious forms from remote tribes. Those
peoples have their own ways of doing things, which make sense to them and are an
organic part of what they do. Their sense of ritual occasion is still fully connected to
how they live. Their ceremonies grow out of the soil directly, and are connected with
food plants or sacred animals. It wouldn't make much sense to uproot their customs
and hope to get a coherent world picture from them right away.

I write this knowing that many people today derive much comfort and wisdom
through their experiences in Native American sweat lodge ceremonies and other in-
digenous-inspired ordeals. The difficulty is not so much accessing the wisdom as being able to live from that place of wisdom when back in the modern world. We need
to look at our own rituals and myths, those things that are around us every day, and
reevaluate them through our understanding of what they represent. I'm suggesting
that rather than steal someone else's roots, we take a moment to rediscover our own.

Looking back at my bewildered schooldays, I'm always surprised that the school
didn't use even the most basic of references to ritual. Of course, we were taught about
the Greeks and Romans, and we were made to read *The Odyssey*; but at no point did
anyone take the next step and suggest that Odysseus's travels might, in some way,
apply to us. In the literal minds of my schoolmasters, Odysseus's struggles, mistakes,
and the important life lessons he learns were merely the stuff of ancient fable. Nor
did they conceive that Odysseus's triumphant return to Ithaca, to take up his rightful
work as king, might be a useful metaphor for us to reflect upon. We were not asked to
connect our own struggles to achieve personal growth to Odysseus's heroic journey.

We could put it another way. In that conventionally observant Church of England school, there was no need to look any farther than Jesus and his 40 days and 40 nights in the wilderness if they wanted to reassure us about difficult transitions. Had our schoolmasters wanted us to reflect on rites of passage at all, that story was certainly easily available for us to examine. Yet they did nothing of the sort; instead, we boys were expected to soldier on with those British stiff upper lips. In other words, most of us had to put on an act in order to survive. And so we became inauthentic even to ourselves.

The Inadequacy of Current Religious Rituals

We must be careful at this point, since there are plenty of religious rituals available that might serve the purposes I've defined. The trouble with such rituals, though, is that more often than not they are concerned with strengthening the power and orthodoxy of religious institutions, rather than encouraging adherents to become more fully themselves or grow in wisdom.

For example, the head of the Catholic Church, the Pope, offers a highly visual example of one sort of religious ceremonial. We see him dressed in immaculate white surrounded by his cardinals in their gorgeous scarlet, gathered in the vast, majestic halls of St. Peter's in Rome amid gold-encrusted monuments. It's a colorful sight, but it is a long way from its origins—the actions of a Jewish carpenter and preacher and a bunch of his followers, who taught simplicity, poverty, and the leveling of religious hierarchies. Their teachings specified that we find the kingdom of God within ourselves, not through an organization.

The rituals of the Church have been, as we know, modified over the centuries to reflect the importance of the institution. The holiness is there, but the machinery of the Church has become too cumbersome for some worshippers to be able to relate to its belief structures fully or directly. Congregations are declining in much of North America as a result.

For exactly these reasons many modern religions have failed us, their truly beautiful messages submerged by dogma.

The Example of Confirmation

Returning once more to my years at that public school, there were many so-called rituals available, but most of them had been devalued by "modern" ways of thinking. First Communions, Confirmations, Bar Mitzvahs, and other religious rituals did, in fact, take place regularly. But they felt empty to most of us. This was, in part, because the adults concerned did not feel their ritual power, so it was impossible for them to communicate it to us.

The priest who performed my own Confirmation was a nice man, but I cannot say the occasion moved me in the way he seemed to hope. Instead, what I most recall of that day is that the ceremony was interrupted by a power workers' strike. All the lights went out. So, on that rainy evening the church staff set about placing candles next to every pew. As a result, what I most remember of the ceremony is the magical flickering light in the church, which by pure accident created an atmosphere of wonder and beauty. The candlelight was also potentially dangerous; we could easily have set our clothes on fire with a careless movement. Those candles were also susceptible to every slight breeze that threatened to blow the tiny flames out, and I can recall we all had to move with a much greater consciousness of our bodies than normal. We had to slow down, and think about how we moved.

I do not recall if my parents were present, or in fact anyone from my family. I do not recall any of the words, prayers, or any of the promises I made. I can only recall the softness of the candlelight and the sense that what was to have been a boring occasion had, by pure chance, been turned into something magical and worth remembering. Something had changed for me. Now I had a story that could help to articulate that.

Most of the ritual points in my early life have been empty rituals, and this feeling is one I hear about very often from my counseling clients. I mention my Confirmation because it accidentally was imbued with magic and beauty. It would have been far more effective for all of us that day if the clergymen had started from beauty, and added in the prayers, rather than focusing on the prayers and forgetting about beauty. By pure chance, the transformative effect of the candlelight allowed my emotions to be engaged. It spoke directly to my heart. For if the emotions are not involved, then the memory cannot last long. We recall what moves us.

Looking back now, I think I know what changed. Instead of this occasion being simply something I did at a particular point in my life, the beauty of the moment and the candlelight connected me to something older. I felt that many generations had gone through this sort of ceremony, in many places, and under many different circumstances. I felt linked to them, even in my ignorance. Just like me, most of those people would not have had the strongest grasp on what was happening. How could they? The whole purpose of a ritual is that we make sense of it afterward, while at the time it may well feel slightly confused. In fact, it is often the confusion that leads us to ask questions—the answers to which are often important, and which only come later upon reflection.

The Importance of Reflection
in this Process

Let's use a different example, but one that has some useful parallels. When I was 24 I trained and took part in my first parachute jumps. I wasn't really convinced that all the things they had drilled into us over the previous training days were that important. I mean, how difficult could it be to throw yourself out of a plane? Between preparatory exercises we all stood around in the drafty aircraft hanger feeling bored, waiting for the rain to ease up.

It wasn't until I was sitting in the open door of the plane at 7,000 feet that I began to understand why it would be important to recall what I'd been told about preparing to jump. Then, the engine roar changed as the small plane eased back on its throttle. It was my turn to sit forward, place my hands in the designated positions, brace, and push. Everything happened very rapidly after that. I remember it all in tremendous detail. I was suddenly very alive to everything.

Even so, the real impact of what I was doing didn't dawn on me right away. That only happened when I landed with a thump and was told immediately to repack my chute and get ready to do it all again. Only when I was ready to repeat it was I forced to reflect on what my first experience could teach me, going forward. Earlier lessons on overcoming fear, facing the unknown, and how we defend ourselves from perceiving real danger suddenly all began to make more sense to me. And they made sense only because I'd already had that startling few minutes, dangling in the air under the canopy of my parachute, in which I felt every part of myself to be fully alive. Moreover, in the days afterward, when I talked with my fellow jumpers, we slowly began to see even deeper lessons in the experience we had just had.

Going into it, I suppose we thought we'd be triumphant, crowing over what we'd done. We thought we'd have the bragging rights. Instead, we found ourselves somewhat humbled, with a renewed respect for our own existences. We'd touched the pitiless elements and felt our fragility. We'd found out the joy of being near the edge. We'd grown up just a bit. Something had changed that I still cannot fully articulate but that I can certainly remember. I remember it best when I tell the story and reengage with the feelings.

This taught me one important thing, at least. The value of ritual is not what you can carry away afterward; it's about how you feel as you go through it.

Perceiving ritual is like watching dancers at long distance. They move in odd and unexpected ways, and perhaps seem beautiful or just crazed. As we come closer, though, and begin to hear the music they are responding to, we begin to feel the rhythm, respond to the melody, and appreciate the movements. We see them moving into harmony, doing something more than just an athletic exercise. We watch as they link to something mythic that we have not yet, perhaps, fully understood, but can feel. We know it's there; and so we move toward myth, too.

Moments of change, moments of wonder, can link us to a larger sense of ourselves and what it means to grow into greater awareness. This awakens us to the mythic aspect of our lives. Rituals force us to let go of our little ego concerns and to experience the mystery, the beauty, and the majesty of the world we live in. When we are awestruck by an event, or moved by its beauty, we cannot deny that there is something bigger than we are that we also are a part of. The only possible reaction to encountering the wonder of our world is gratitude—gratitude that we are alive, experiencing what we feel. When we feel this we are living from the heart, not from the head, and we connect with the energies of the greater universe. For it is our heart's knowledge that will truly guide us through our lives, not those carefully finessed half-truths the ego will work out for us.

The ritual event requires—demands—that we be fully present; when we are, we will know we are part of a larger "story" about what it means to be human. That story is the mythic dimension. If you take the trouble to notice how you feel about the events of your life, you'll experience myth everywhere. With myth, life becomes resonant. For it is only when we can perceive the underlying patterns and structures of life that we can begin to find our true place in the world.

CHAPTER FOUR

So What Do We Do?
One Size Does Not Fit All

For those who have read this far and expect an answer—some sort of simple solution to the problem of the absence of myth—I have some bad news: I'm not going to tell you exactly what to do. This is not because I'm withholding an answer; I'm not. In fact, I'll be making some practical suggestions that will help you see your way forward. It is not my intention to leave you without specific guidance but to lead you toward a deeper awareness from which guidance will emerge

I have a specific reason for not being prescriptive. I'm aware that every person reading this is going to need his or her own way of creating a ritual space and practice, and that, to some extent, each of us must be free to choose the myth that best suits our needs. Religions are usually quite good at helping us with this, telling us what to do in a gentle way—at least, at first. They let each person chose a saint or holy man to emulate, as long as that person is not too outlandish, then they ask us to join in certain shared celebrations in our public worship.

The point is that ritual space is going to be slightly different for everyone, and we must be free to create that for ourselves. For some people, sacred space can only be in a chapel or temple. For others, it must be out in nature or in an art gallery or museum. For still others, there may be corners of the home where pictures are placed—perhaps images of family members—where anyone may contemplate the nature of family, duty, love, and attachment. For the creative person, the act of creation—the steady habit of going into the studio or study to do creative work—may feel every bit as vital a contact with the divine as any other experience.

There are no rules, but there are some basic understandings. The first is that we be mindful of what moves us to connect with the eternal, and to see ourselves as more than merely part of the daily struggle to survive and gain wealth.

Organized religions tend to want us to follow rules; they demand that we go to the holy place on certain days, or several times each day, and that the "real" holy experience is the one relayed to us by the priest, minister, imam, or specific functionary of the faith.

Rumi, the 13th-century Sufi poet (and, therefore, a person who had broken away from orthodox Islam), expresses this well:

> Don't be satisfied with stories,
> How things have gone with others.
> Unfold your own myth
> Without complicated explanation.[1]

We are here to find our own sense of holiness and ritual, not to buy into anyone else's without thinking.

The Buddha's Temple

A story is told about the Buddha as he lay on his deathbed that may illustrate this idea further. Knowing he was about to die, the story goes, one of his disciples asked the Buddha what sort of temple should be raised to him. The Buddha, ever inscrutable, simply took his wooden begging bowl and placed it upside down on the earth.

Everyone present noted this and nodded wisely. Later, this gave rise to some extended arguments, because one set of his followers interpreted the action to mean that there should be no temples, since the bowl was empty. Another group protested that what the Buddha had signaled, obviously, was that he wanted temples in the shape of upturned begging bowls—and, indeed, many were constructed with exactly that sort of dome on them. You can see them to this day. For a while there was fierce contention as to which was the correct way to proceed.

Yet, if we're alert, there is a third option open. The Buddha must have known that anything he said would be misinterpreted by someone, and he knew that those who wanted and needed temples would have to have them, and wouldn't be happy until they did. Those who didn't want or need temples wouldn't create them. *Ultimately it makes no difference which path anyone chooses because they all end up at the same place.* Everyone forms a spiritual practice in his or her own way, and the only thing that matters is that the spiritual practice happens, not what its ultimate form is. It's a beautiful story about the wisdom of the Buddha—a myth in its own right—and it reveals an important truth about human spiritual needs. His deliberately ambivalent answer was less a solution than a description.

So what does this mean in practical terms? What do we do?

The most important point to notice in this story from the Buddha's life is that he doesn't say we are to ignore rituals or throw them away. On the contrary, he seems to be saying that we should pay attention to them, honor them, and see them as existing on several levels simultaneously. At one level, he suggests we can choose an actual temple in a specific shape if that feels necessary for our devotions. At the next level, he suggests that we may not need a temple at all. And at the highest level he offers us an insight into the ways we can make meaning, when we ourselves become the temple. Depending upon where we are in our awareness, we may need one of these ways of seeing things as a place to start.

Most of us, especially when young, need a special place, a temple, where we can have our own space. As we grow we can make that quiet space for ourselves without being tied to a specific location. Seen this way, the temple we choose is not an end in itself; it is simply a path toward a spiritual experience, and so it has to be taken seriously. We can have a deeply spiritual experience in a Spanish cathedral or in a Himalayan cave or under a railway arch in London. The place doesn't matter very much in itself, but it does matter as a way of helping us to get to that experience. We can achieve the state that will feed our spiritual hunger *only* by having reverence for *every* ritual level that is positive.

In order to do that we'll need to learn how to think in terms of ritual and myth, so that we can connect with the deep meanings life offers us so plentifully. That's exactly what we'll be doing.

In the following pages, I'll be giving you some examples of secular rituals to think about, so that you can see how they function, the power they hold, and also how sometimes they can be less than healthy. In the end, armed with this new awareness, it'll be up to you to choose whichever myths speak to you. But, if this book succeeds, what I hope will happen is that you will begin to see the ritual aspects that are already present in your life. You'll see them with new eyes, or perhaps for the very first time, and as a result you will attune yourself with the mythic dimensions of existence. Those dimensions are already there. We just have to learn how to see them.

The formula I'd suggest is simple: Whatever causes us to be more aware of the mystery, the beauty, and our sense of deep connection with the world is what we should move toward. We can do it however we like, but we *must* do it. This action will move us toward the place in which we listen to what our heart is telling us, not our head. Perhaps yoga does this for you, or meditation. Perhaps stargazing or standing beside a river, fishing. Perhaps tending to a grandchild or weeding a garden. Whatever you choose as a ritual activity is fine as long as you realize why you are choosing it. That knowledge is all that is required.

For all these reasons, we won't be spending a lot of time excavating early Greek and Roman stories and analyzing them. Plenty of books already exist that do that extremely well. To some extent they suggest that myth is far away and long ago. It isn't. Myths and rituals are present right here and now, but we have lost sight of them. When we see them clearly, when we understand how they do what they do, we will find that all rituals are linked in a specific way.

Ritual, as we will see, has several aspects. The first might be that a moment of beauty or wonder lets us contact our sense of the divine. When we do that we are aware that this moment is different from what we had thought of as ordinary life. The second aspect is that when we experience this special moment we realize that we have changed. We are no longer who we once were. So, a man who sees a field of flowers and marvels at them has a moment of encountering the divine. If he then goes back, regularly, to look at flowers and feel the same way again, he has created a personal ritual. And when he does that he will never again think of nature as inconsequential. The personal moment actually marks a point of change and growth. Rituals large and small always mark change points in our lives.

At the end of this book, when we've seen how to differentiate between genuine and false rituals, we will find that all the genuine myths, legends, stories, and rituals are in support of the same thing. They mark the points of change in a schema of human spiritual growth that is as old as anything we know. They connect to the deep archetypal structures that exist in all of us, and have done since recorded time, serving as ways to show us how we can grow. Rituals and myths are the surface ripples on a deep river, which is carrying us along.

Before we can consider this in detail, though, we'll have to understand the situation thoroughly.

PART II

The Advantages Of Ritual: Learning To Listen To Your Heart

In a lively bedroom conversation between the two lovers in Ali Smith's hilarious best-selling novel Girl Meets Boy, *Anthea asks whether myths spring "fully formed from the imagination and needs of a society's subconscious," or whether they are created by "money-making forces." Her question alerts us to important aspects of myth exploration. It suggests that there are two kinds of myth: the deep variety that comes from the subconscious and which exists to articulate its needs to us, and the kind created by commercial interests.*

Ali Smith goes on to tell us in no uncertain terms that, one way or another, we all have myths swirling around us and to be aware of that. When Anthea claims to have grown up "mythless" Robin is quick to correct her, saying, "Nobody grows up mythless… It's what we do with the myths we grow up with that matters." [1]

So what can healthy ritual and myth really give us? And how do we shape our own lives so we can attend to our soul hunger? We'll be addressing these questions in this section.

First and foremost, when we become aware of a ritual or a mythic aspect to our lives it causes us to pause, and in so doing, we become more mindful of the basic fact that we are human beings who have lives that are not confined by the deadlines and demands that are forced on us. Stories remind us that we are not the only people who have ever felt this way about something. Knowing this, we are immediately less isolated with just our swirling thoughts for company.

In that moment when we stop our busy work, we are able to allow ourselves to feel gratitude for simply being alive. Doing this, we perceive our lives as not being about the ego—about me, me, me—but, rather, about our connection to others. Real myth connects; commercial myth isolates. And so it is that when we listen to real myth and engage in powerful ritual, it allows us to listen to our hearts. What our hearts tell us is that we are all linked, if only we would look below the surface. This is our center place.

CHAPTER FIVE

The Nature of Ritual and Myth

The nature of ritual is that it transforms an object into a subject, an ordinary event into something special. So eating food is simply an event, but sharing food can be a representation of communion, an event as culturally important as taking Communion in the Christian mass. Washing one's face is a mundane fact, yet when Muslims at prayer make a movement that closely resembles face-washing while admitting their faults to Allah, we have something that has far more resonance. Ritual can link our actions to a deeper underlying structure of meaning and, in the process, bring us into contact with that meaning. It thus adds a dimension to our lives.

Having observed Muslim prayers and the face-washing action, I never fail now to think about what that might mean for Muslims. I think of it whenever I wash my own face. The ordinary action now has an added dimension for me. Similarly, a set of fluttering ribbons may mean very little, but under certain circumstances they take on the attributes of a national flag—the red, white, and blue, for example—with all the attendant feelings of belonging and pride.

Ritual elevates the ordinary to the mystical. At the center of every ritual is gratitude—gratitude for being alive, gratitude for the love or the presence of others. And so it places us in a relationship to the divine that is essentially loving. It reaffirms this vital link.

Myths, since they are usually stories narrated rather than acted out, are the next stage removed from these habits of action. They allow us to discuss the stories that exist behind the actions (as we might perhaps discuss the Bible, or any other religious or literary document). So myths work to move our awareness to a more general and external level. Myth is capable of being just as powerful as ritual, but it is different. Rituals show us what our connection to the divine is; myths tell us how to talk about it.

If we return for a moment to the start of this book, we can see that rituals are almost always about accessing courage. They are a way of talking about what will happen to us and managing the approach to it so that we're not frightened. This can go awry, too. Those people who have all sorts of weird and superstitious actions that they must do in order to face each day might be trying to control what they are afraid of rather than facing it. That's the unhealthy side of ritual, yet it arises spontaneously in everyday life, indicating how important it is. It tells us that we need ritual, and we need someone to help us find the healthiest version of what a ritual is.

The Mountain Lion

Let me give an example. A student of mine from New York City told a story about how she was staying in a motel in Colorado and opened her door one morning to find a mountain lion standing 10 feet away in the corridor. It snarled, and she shut the door fast. She grabbed the phone and called reception. "There's a mountain lion right outside my door!" she screamed. "Yup, ma'am," said the calm voice at the other end, "them mountain lions do like to come inside and look around some. I'll ask someone to open the fire door so he can get out easy. He'll be gone soon." Half an hour later she steeled herself and opened the door. The lion was gone.

No one at the motel was surprised by her story. The encounter had changed her attitude, though. She saw that in this wild place she was the intruder into the lion's domain, and she had better get used to that. Like those boys dragged from the women's compound we mentioned earlier, she had seen something that placed her in a different relationship to her world.

Now, it's not a big thing, perhaps, but if, when she'd called reception, five men with rifles had come stampeding to her help, do you think she could have learned the same lesson? I don't think so. She'd simply have learned fear. She'd have learned that nature was "other"—dangerous—and needed to be taken care of in decisive and destructive ways. She might even have been traumatized by the event. As it was, she learned respect and wonder, as well as about the beauty of a mountain lion's movements and its snarl. She'd learned respect for Nature, with a capital N.

Had this woman grown up in rural Colorado, she would undoubtedly have learned such lessons as a matter of course. She'd have seen dangerous creatures, probably while quite young and in the company of a competent adult, and learned to regulate her fear. As it turned out, she had to learn her lesson in the way we've described. For her the important moment came when she apologized to the person at reception and he smiled and said that she needn't apologize. This sort of thing just wasn't what "city folks" were used to, he said. What she most appreciated, she said, was the calm acceptance that *of course* she'd been afraid, and *of course* she wouldn't have to be afraid in that way any more. It was just fear, it was natural, and now it was over. In that moment, the fear was no longer overpowering. It was simply a fact to be dealt with. In those few minutes she began to access her courage as well as her sense of wonder for the natural world around her. She began to feel, for the first time, the beauty that was the lion.

She was fortunate. The calm and reasonable person at reception had understood the human situation right away and recognized a learning opportunity, a growth point—although he probably wouldn't have expressed it that way. It's a moment when we say: "Oh yes, I remember how scary that felt for me, too. It's okay. There's no criticism here. It's just the way the world works."

What we're considering here is such moments of change, their emotional power, and their connection to rituals, large and small, that we've lost. They are worth reclaiming.

The case I'm making is this: Everything, every human situation you live through, is unique to your life, but every human action has been seen before in its general outlines. If we make the mistake of thinking that our experience of life is unique, then we cannot learn from what others have seen and done before us. But if we accept that our life path is one others have been on, then we can ask literature and myth and ritual for guidance, since that is exactly why these stories were written down and why the meaningful actions persisted over the centuries. They were created to let us know that we are not alone. Others have been this way before. This is what they did when faced with similar situations. At such times we can't be taken by surprise by events, or least not for very long.

Better yet is that we realize that almost everything has significance when we live the life of myth; everything is an opportunity for more understanding, more connection. Today's disaster may be difficult, but it will be part of a larger picture, which may lift us higher. This wider perspective can be enormously helpful. It reduces our little ego concerns and replaces them with a powerful sense of ourselves as part of a larger, more meaningful whole.

To understand this, let's look at the experience of Tayo, the Native American main character of Leslie Marmon Silko's novel *Ceremony*, as he begins to feel a renewed sense of wonder and deep connection to the myths of his culture that he had temporarily lost:

> Everywhere he looked, he saw a world made of stories, the long
> ago, time immemorial stories, as old Grandma called them. It
> was a world alive, always changing and moving; and if you knew
> where to look, you could see it, sometimes almost imperceptible,
> like the motion of the stars across the sky.[1]

It's a wonderful description of a world suddenly revealing its fullness of meaning. This is exactly what we are considering. In my groups and workshops I've often been fortunate to have people write and speak movingly about precisely the sort of experience my student had with the mountain lion. We've shared tales of encounters with everything from moose and bears to the bleak sense of being stuck alone on top of a mountain peak in a blizzard.

What emerges from such stories is a powerful sense of having encountered something far bigger and other than ourselves, of a humbling experience that has, at the same time, let us know something about our true place in the world, when the daily ego concerns drop away. These are holy moments, *because we will never be the same afterward*. We will be transformed, if we allow ourselves to be. The eagerness with which people talk and write also tells me something else—that these sorts of experiences are not accepted or valued by others in "normal" life. Because of this, sometimes we cannot contact their power.

The Swim to Safety

Consider this example. A young woman wrote and talked about a time when, as a very young child, a rising tide had cut her off from the safe route home. Her older brother was with her, and as the dark waters (she described them as "black") began to rise, he got her to put her arms around his neck and climb on his back. Then he swam with her, around the rocky point to the beach beyond, skirting the dark rocks pounded by the waves. Can you visualize that? Can you feel it? The woman, now in her twenties, shed tears as she recalled that moment, when she was perhaps five, and frightened. She didn't mind dying, she said, as long as she could be with her brother.

We could analyze all this, of course, and put it into reasonable prose with technical terms and psychological footnotes. Or we could wonder at it, and *feel* it. This event had become for her a defining story about so many things—who she could rely on, her fear of death, her confrontation of that fear, and so on. She'd felt the power of the threat of death, and also that there was something stronger: human beings caring for each other… love. But it was also so much more.

These two events—the mountain lion and the swim to safety—may seem very different, but they were both occasions when a threat was faced and a rite of passage achieved. The difference is that one participant was an adult, who had other adults to help her "hold" the event after it happened, while the second was an adventure shared only by two children who never spoke of it to anyone in the family afterward.

In the example of the mountain lion, the other adults knew how to receive and validate the information, so it became part of a ritual process that honored the event. In contrast, the young swimmer felt her experience was something she did not quite know how to deal with, and it left her feeling more alone until, years later, she could talk about it. Only then could she see that this was an encounter with death, one that had alerted her to the strength of her own sense of what it meant to be alive. It became mythic at that point, when it was shared.

The Difference Between
Isolation and Sharing

Here's another example, one that we've all felt, I'm sure. It may help to explain the example I've just given. If we regard death as the end, then we have to admit it's not a very happy situation. Perhaps we'll be frightened by it. But what if we regard death as an inevitable part of life? What if we see that what matters is not how much we gained materially in this life but whether we set anything good or joyous or loving in motion that will remain after we're dead?

If we allow ourselves to see things this way, then death becomes a different proposition entirely. Dying merely becomes the point at which we step off the train of life, knowing that the train will continue, and that the other passengers we know and grew to love while we were rattling down the tracks will take some part of us with them as the journey unrolls. Our contribution will endure.

That may seem like a big claim, so I'll simply refer to history to support it. Despite everything the newspapers tell us, certain aspects of our world are improving. Three hundred years ago most of the world was in a state of perpetual war, and the average life expectancy was 40 years. This is not an exaggeration. There were wars large and small everywhere, and most people lived in houses that were barred and shuttered at night. Lawlessness at all levels was the rule. Today we live in a society in which wars continue to wreak their havoc, but at nothing like the rate of previous centuries. Bit by bit the world is becoming more civilized and more loving.

This movement toward a better society, however, is under threat because the very understandings that allowed for growing cohesion have been eroded recently. They've been undercut by those who cannot see that there is any value in belonging to a society of more than one, who do not see any continuity. Their lives are just for them, and there is no sense of the mythic richness of being alive. They have no "story" to connect them to their culture, and so they have no sense of ritual; they have no awareness of history, merely of isolated occurrences.

If events are simply random, if other people are just objects to be networked with, or even exploited, then how can the person who thinks like that respond to any higher levels of awareness? These are the people who cannot find any deep significance in their lives, so they grab what they can of the material world and of physical gratification. This is the saddest aspect of modern isolation.

The consciousness that we are living a mythic life, where right and wrong actions have significance, and where we are all linked, is the best response to this every-man-for-himself mindset. We can choose to see ourselves as part of a meaningful whole, where our actions matter. In the process we grow our courage to live well.

The Next Step

So far, we have looked at ritual as a stepping stone, a moment of recognition or an occasion that links us to the sense of where we stand in the cosmic order. This is, for many of us, something that is validated by our specific society. It keeps us in harmony with those around us. Some of these moments of recognition are already familiar to us. If we want to think historically, all the great and ancient festivals of the harvest and the equinoxes, which occurred in every civilization from the earliest times, are a way of reminding people that they are part of the cycle of the seasons, part of the divine creativity of the earth. This gives us a sense of our place in the world we inhabit and a feeling of gratitude for what the earth provides. But there is more.

When we find ourselves accepting the value of these rituals, something important happens: we choose to live by listening to our hearts, not our egos. A ritual is just an event, ultimately, unless we connect to it with our hearts and imaginations. If we enter this heart space, where we see we are inextricably part of all that surrounds us, we move toward doing what is right and good and humane. We become part of a mythic structure, a series of understandings about goodness and generosity.

If we listen to the heart it will always tell us to take the loving option. And at that point we find ourselves aligning with the powers that created the universe, waiting for what they need us to do. It's not about what we want any more; it's about what we're here to contribute.

For example: I may say I want a big fast car. That's my ego talking, because I certainly don't *need* one. But I also know that I'm not on earth to roar around the roads making a spectacle of myself. My heart tells me there are much better things to do, things that will bring far finer and deeper satisfactions. One of the most important of these is the serious business of loving and accepting other people. We are all linked, so I cannot actually *not* love others without making an artificial split between "me" and "them."

Now, if I accept this connection and follow my heart's prompting it will lead me to a place of harmony and, ultimately, synchronicity. Synchronicity is best described as what occurs when we are aligned with the energy of the universe and doing its will. That is when things happen for us, seemingly miraculously—the impossible becomes possible. Living like this takes a huge amount of trust, since so many people will tell us this is merely chance, or luck, or a delusion. But it isn't; it is far more than that.

And the more we trust it the stronger we become, so we are better able to respond to the synchronicities we receive.

I have written about this extensively in my previous book *The Path of Synchronicity* (Findhorn Press, 2011), where I outline the process in more detail. Even if you choose not to believe synchronicity exists, I think you will agree that moving into harmony with our fellow creatures is a good notion if we are to survive.

The thing I'd like you to consider, here, is the *process*. Ritual can wake us up to the wonder that is our world; it then alerts us to the presence of the myths we live by, which keep our social networks together. This is good. It helps us to be more loving. We give to charity, we help our neighbors and relatives, and we act as part of a caring social structure because, at their best, that is what human beings do.

Knowing this can lead us to the next stage: the place of being a willing instrument for wherever the universe needs. Sometimes it can be as simple as saying, "Well, somebody's got to do it" and rolling our sleeves up. After all, we are here to make things better for us all. If we listen to our hearts, we will be able to find out what we have to do. And that place is where synchronicity occurs. When it happens we know it. At such times it feels as if we cannot put a foot wrong, and we find deep joy in being in that space.

That's when we know we are living authentically from the heart.

CHAPTER SIX

Myth Doesn't Have to Be True to Reveal Truth

About now, it might be a good idea to take a few steps back from this discussion and try to spell out what a ritual is and what a myth might be. A ritual can be anything that one does to mark an event, to commemorate it. The important thing is that the form of the ritual has to have some consistency over time.

So an ordinary cake becomes a birthday cake by the addition of candles, and a turkey is just a turkey until Thanksgiving Day puts it into a context of some sort, and these are actions that are fairly consistently controlled. The contexts can change, of course, and obscure the event that is supposed to be remembered. Christmas becomes, for some people, simply a time to buy gifts rather than a time to think about the tenets of a specific religious or spiritual idea.

In comparison, a myth is more complicated. Its focus is not the action that is taken so much as the story that describes a period of time in a figure's life—often a figure who is not a normal mortal—from which we are invited to draw certain lessons about our own lives.

The myth of Adam and Eve's banishment from Eden was used by the Christian Church to show that mankind is inherently selfish and that we must fight against this feeling. This is called "original sin." The story was used for many other purposes as well, but that is a basic interpretation within the Church. The myth explains the tendency of people to behave badly, according to the Church's version of things, and prescribes what we ought to be doing instead. It directs life into social channels. A different interpretation of the myth would produce a different series of insights, of course, which would either be accepted by the dominant social systems, or rejected as inaccurate.

In contrast, a ritual is a physical experience that reinforces a physical action, giving it emphasis. The rituals of marriage and making vows are there to show, in public, that two people wish to be together; the occasion makes the feelings manifest to all. When each person in the happy couple feels nervous, excited, and slightly dazed it is often a huge relief to have those swirling feelings publicly acknowledged, too. The guests laugh and are happy and make jokes about it, and everyone admits that this series of feelings is entirely to be expected at such an emotionally laden moment.

The ritual cherishes the couple's feelings in all their complexity and seeks to guide the young people forward. Left to their own devices they might get cold feet and back out. The ritual helps them to see that there is a way forward and that nervousness is natural, even healthy. The ritual "holds" the event so that the emotions do not derail it.

Weddings can get bogged down, as we all know, in confused considerations about display, dresses, flowers, and so on. This is very often just another way of showing nervousness, and the ritual paraphernalia of bouquets and banquets can be a way of centering that free-floating anxiety. This nervousness, though, is always about recognizing the importance of the moment. With luck, the real importance will be seen not as being just about the flowers but as being about spiritual value. The flowers or food will be seen as simply the vehicle to express this, but we have to be alert or we'll see the wrong things.

When the totality of this experience is seen in the cultural context of what marriage is generally agreed to be, then the happy couple accepts the myth of marriage, as defined by their society. They take on all the responsibilities involved and subscribe to the full meaning of "being married" as the appropriate physical and spiritual expression of who they now are. In a perfect world that would be a spiritual step forward. Of course, many marriages don't make it to that point.

Ritual and myth are, therefore, invitations to all concerned to go beyond the surface meaning and find a deep resonance. For many people today that alone is an unfamiliar idea: some people do not like to look deeply into anything, while others like to look deeply at the wrong things.

Believers in strange conspiracy theories are those who are looking for deeper meanings, too, but usually in order to confirm their own deepest fears and prejudices about the way the world is being mishandled or the truth is being concealed. This is the same impulse that moves us toward the deep meanings of myth, but it has lost its way and serves to raise anxiety rather than to give a sense of connectedness. The aim of myth is always to reveal an aspect of truth, even if that truth is hard to apprehend. The aim of ritual is to make the truth tangible, experiential—to act it out.

Plato and Myth

Ted Hughes, the late British poet laureate, had a number of interesting things to add to this idea about myth. Hughes points to Plato's *Republic*, where the Greek philosopher states that myths are valuable for their ability to inform the citizens about eternal truths; Plato felt that these stories were an essential component of the New

Republic. This is surprising because Plato, otherwise, wanted to exclude poets entirely, since he saw them as not telling the truth![1]

The point we need to recall about Plato is that, perhaps surprisingly, he did not believe the accepted myths of his society to be true, and neither did most of his contemporaries. They didn't believe in those mythological creatures any more than most people today do.

Remember, this was a society that was surprisingly advanced. For example, in about 240 B.C., Eratosthenes of Cyrene had already accurately calculated the circumference of the globe. He also successfully estimated the distance of the earth from the moon. This was not a man who would believe that the sun was a blazing chariot that flew across the heavens every day, drawn by fiery steeds, which is what the myths said was the case. Instead, what Plato and his contemporaries recognized was that monsters and heroes and myths are the expressions of psychic needs, made into stories.

The valuable stories—the ones that somehow reflected something vital about human life and emotional states—survived; the rest tended to be forgotten because they had no real emotional or spiritual resonance. It was this spiritual resonance, the myths as metaphors, which was of interest to Plato. That's a rather startlingly modern response. Centaurs and dragons and so on were to be seen as part of stories that had captured the imagination, like dreams. The myths were the language of the unconscious expressing itself. Then, once these tales existed as images, they could be discussed.

Let me give you another parallel here. The story of Jesus is widely known and can easily be discussed with reference to all its episodes. In fact the very word Jesus, when brought into a conversation, can prove to have so many different values that it's very hard to know where the discussion starts or ends. Each generation has a slightly different interpretation of Jesus and his life, and while some interpretations stay with us others are allowed to fade out.

Whether Jesus existed or not, and whether one is Christian or not, matters less than that by knowing the story we can reflect on standards of conduct and on spiritual verities we feel but cannot otherwise easily explore. So there are two levels to any myth. First, the feeling has to be cast into the form of a story of some sort, so it can be grasped. Second, once the story has been grasped, it can be talked about, examined, and perhaps treasured for its richness. It can't be talked about, though, until it exists in a form, such as a myth.

Seen in this way it does not matter in the slightest if a myth is "true." What matters is that it should be seen as a way of approaching the truth.

Here is another example. When you visit some Buddhist temples you may well see there are two large ogres placed at the entrance. Huge sculpted forms—30 feet high, perhaps—guard the entrance and glower at those who approach. No one actually believes these guardians will threaten anyone, because anyone who has any sense can see they are simply statues. Not even children seem scared of them. The statues, though, remind us that as we approach the shrine we have to let go of those fears we have for our earthly concerns, like physical well-being. The *image* is that only a brave person can move safely past ogres, and that when we use our courage imagined ogres become as unthreatening as mere inanimate objects; yet the *meaning* is spiritual.

In this sense both rituals and myths are vulnerable, because people could easily laugh at them as being fantastic, silly, juvenile. People have discounted the Grimm brothers' fairy tales for exactly the same reason, relegating to the nursery what was once a serious body of knowledge discussed carefully by thoughtful adults.

As I examined in detail in my earlier book, *Princes, Frogs and Ugly Sisters* (Findhorn Press, 2010), the Grimm brothers' tales cover profound psychological issues, such as incest, parental neglect, attempted rape, victimization, narcissism, and so on.[2] They provide a language that enabled generations of Europeans as intelligent as any of us to talk about what they had noticed so they could decide what could be done to remedy the situation. The stories, related with careful exactitude by traveling storytellers, in a ritualistic setting (perhaps around a hearth at night), claimed the imagination. They also upheld cultural values about proper and healthy behavior, and so became part of a mythic structure of beliefs. Now this process is almost entirely extinct.

The great mythologist Joseph Campbell was sensitive to this situation. He suggested that the best way forward was to create new myths that would feel true today. He thought this was the role of the poets and artists of our civilization. He heaped praise on James Joyce for producing a modern myth in his masterpiece *Ulysses*, and he praised W. B. Yeats for his re-creation of the old Celtic myths. These are important writers, truly; however, I suspect Campbell may have been mistaken in his belief that these writers provided alternative myths. I suspect that the "truth" of myth was never an issue.

I have no way of proving this objectively, since one would have to go back in time and ask them, but I would be surprised if the earliest readers of what is now the Old Testament of the Bible (and, therefore, of the Torah) actually objectively believed that the earth and everything in it was created in six days. What they did know was that the story reflected the wonder that is our earth, and so allowed them to apprehend and understand it just a little more fully. The story of the six days of creation and the seventh day of rest gave them a shape to their lives, a rhythm of work and rest that they could hold on to. This was practical and necessary. But the sense of wonder was what made it all special, what made the working days feel valuable.[3]

The six days of creation set up a hierarchy, orders of magnitude by which we could think of our existence. So for example, the division of light and darkness, on day one, tells us about the vast energies of the universe. It reminds us that since mankind was created later, we must not think that we are the most important things ever created. But who makes that connection today? We don't need new myths. We need once again to become familiar with the old ones.

This, after all, is the language of dreams. When we dream, we accept the rules of that world even as we wonder about them. Oh, I can fly in this dream? Okay, let's see where I can go. . . Talking about these dreams later, we may begin to identify themes of freedom that the imagery of flying suggests to us. Most of our dreams are not literally "true" in this waking world to which we return, but that doesn't mean we value them less. It certainly doesn't mean they are without value. In some cases, the value we perceive is actually enhanced by the unrealistic nature of these visions.

Test yourself with this, right now. Can you think of dreams you have had that you've dreamed more than once? Can you think of dreams that have stayed in your memory for a while? Most people report that they can, even if they have only a fleeting sense of those dreams; it's rare to find someone who doesn't recall anything.

Sometimes, people remember dreams they had decades ago—they can bring them to mind in great detail. Sometimes, a dream or a part of a dream will recur throughout a person's life. People don't forget these things, no matter how their daytime lives unfold, and no matter what else they forget. We'll recall a dream, yet forget the password to a website or where we left our keys. We both "believe" in the dream and recognize it as "only" a dream. Myth works the same way.

Think of that when we consider that most compelling of dreams: Dr. Martin Luther King Jr.'s "I have a dream" speech. Think of how it inspired and mobilized people. Yet it was only a dream, right? Images received in dreams and meditations or on vision quests are peculiarly potent for most people.

Moving Beyond Orthodoxy

For our purposes we can now extract some useful things from this discussion. Instead of anyone thinking that his or her religious views are "right" and others' are lacking, we must all try to see beyond the obvious and recognize, in every case, that whatever story we come up with it is about trying to apprehend the wonder that is our world. If we stick with that, we don't have to worry too much about what form the beliefs may take. We simply have to be grateful they exist. Some people, after all, see no wonder at all in the world around us. Grow that sense of wonder and see what a difference it makes.

In my workshops I see people doing this every day. Young and old alike refuse to attach to a specific religion or belief system, and freely take what they need, and what they feel to be vital and true, from many different spiritual traditions. They select what makes sense to them. This is what happens when the deep, personal language of the soul chooses the manner in which to express itself.

Myth, literature, fable, dream, and story—all these are, to a degree, the ways that the preverbal emotions and insights that exist inside each individual can express themselves and find form. If they feel true and vital, then these stories are accepted by others and become the language that those in need can use in order to reflect upon that inner turmoil. This language comes from an inner world that is not always, or even at all, in tune with the outer, rational world. The stories become, therefore, mediators between the two worlds we each live in, and such mediators help to keep us sane. We live simultaneously in both worlds.

CHAPTER SEVEN

How Ritual Can Put Us
In Touch With the Present

What we see when we observe people in sports who refuse to wash a particular sweater, or who go through a complicated process placing special objects in special places, may seem like the worst sort of superstition, but we need to be careful here. This is because any sort of ritualized behavior can, if used with care, help the person to be more fully alert to the present moment. When we are fully present in this way it helps us relax from our swirl of daily thoughts and access our own centered energies.

The lucky rabbit's foot probably does not "bring" luck. That piece of fur is used to get the individual into a place of personal confidence, a mind space that is not the usual, slightly fragmented one we all have. When we're in that special mind space we're more capable of seeing opportunities as they open up on the field of play. We're more alert and confident. I'm sure you can see how easily the routine slips into the mere repetition of rote actions; yet, at their core, each can do the same job. Our task here is to redeem the devalued superstition, the mere repeated action, and replace it with a deeply felt connection.

When T. S. Eliot wrote *The Cocktail Party,* (first staged in 1949), what he was doing, in part, was showing that behind a social ritual such as a drinks party there was often a substantial ritual taking place. It was an occasion in which community was celebrated, along with the acceptance of others. Beyond that lay an acknowledgment that what shields us from hopelessness is being able to love and be loved by other frail and needy human beings. It's a poignant message—one that sums up all that is beautiful and miraculous and terribly fragile about being alive. When we see an event this way, symbolically we move beyond judgments about who is there. It's not about boring old Mr. X and silly Ms. Y, but about all of us being in a similar situation where we can become compassionate. The party is no longer "a success" or "a drag," and it's certainly not about whether the food was better than at someone else's party.[1]

Jane Austen is famous for this sort of implicit comment, which is part of what makes her a great writer. In *Emma*, when Emma Woodhouse unthinkingly mocks the impoverished and aging Miss Bates, it is an offense against the social order that requires compassion for the less fortunate. The value of the ritual is revealed to us because someone carelessly destroys it.

There are plenty of other examples, if we care to look for them. In my father's memoir of the Second World War, he describes having been marched across a freezing Germany in January 1945, expecting to be shot by the guards any day.[2] At a certain point, he finds himself constructing his sleeping place for the night—each prisoner would dig a shallow pit, pile the turf on the windward side, then sleep in the trench and hope the snow wouldn't bury them.

In his diary recording those difficult days, he describes having built his pit for the night, then brewing up a hot drink for himself and his three marching companions. His description? He says he was "perfectly happy" to be with his friends, enjoying a hot cup of something resembling tea. Perfectly happy? It wasn't the ghastly situation that mattered—people freezing to death, Hitler youth boys wanting to shoot them, and so on; it was the deep pleasure of being with companions. That transcended everything. It was a moment of something far more valuable than the hell that was all around them.

That's an example of moving past the present and into the mythic. My father had joined the ranks of Jason and the Argonauts, of Odysseus and his sailors, although I'm sure he didn't think in those terms. He'd found something that was stronger even than the threat of death. That tin cup of something resembling tea was far more than just a hot drink. It was a touching of the eternal—something to equal any Japanese tea ceremonial.

From these instances we can extract what we need to enrich our own lives. When we join any social gathering we can now make a point of seeing it not as a "duty" or as something we're expected to do; instead, we can try to see it as a chance to reaffirm the social bonds we have with those whom perhaps we do not know very well, but who are worthy of respect and acknowledgment because we are all part of the world we inhabit. And if a neighbor is difficult or dull, we can see it as a chance to grow our compassion. One day I, too, may be difficult or ornery, for reasons that may seem valid to me at the time. I may need the compassion I try to give. So often, what we give is exactly what we need to receive—and we can only get it by giving it.

PART III

How To See Beneath The Surface: Some Practical Examples Of Rituals And Myths In Action

Up to this point we've looked at rituals and myths to see how they function. The main point we have established is that understanding the mythic background and its context redeems the power of the ritual. Understanding, however, requires us to practice looking at rituals and decoding them. This next section will help with that task.

> *"The function of Ritual is to give form to human life,*
> *not in the way of mere surface arrangement, but in depth."*
> **—JOSEPH CAMPBELL**

CHAPTER EIGHT

The Mythic Landscape: The World Is Our Sacred Dwelling Place

Joseph Campbell famously observed that to early man everything in the landscape was mythic. When the sun came up it wasn't a call to join the rush hour and get through traffic to the office; it was the ferocious Sun God revisiting the earth to warm it and make it productive for mankind again. I think you can see the difference. The world was personalized, and at the same time mythologized.

When Christianity came to Europe it took over the existing seasonal ceremonies associated with agriculture, then gave them added Christian significance. So Easter, a time of resurrection, was set at the time of rebirth in nature, replacing the pre-Christian fertility celebrations valuing the seasonal cycles of each year. The Christian Church simply decided it would be the rebirth of their particular god as well, and gradually overlaid the first ritual with the newer one of the death and rebirth of Jesus. At around the same time many of the ancient stone circles were taken over, and some of the sites were turned into churches. In such places as Le Mans in France, you can still find the ancient stone menhirs incorporated into the cathedral walls, visible to those who still valued the pagan rites but indubitably now part of the Church.

This process of personalizing the world and at the same time mythologizing it is a primal one, as well as being extremely ancient. It's also with us today, if we care to look.

Personalizing Objects in Our World

We can perhaps begin to understand this if we examine that most modern of phenomena: the man who restores his classic car. When he looks at it, he doesn't just see the shiny but aged automobile. What he sees is all the hours he put into the restoration. He sees a thing of beauty and worth into which he has put enormous amounts of effort and love. He sees a tradition of manufacture, perhaps even a history lesson of events and evolving design. Perhaps he calls it by a pet name. And yet he also knows that it is a car, not new, and that there are perhaps thousands of others just like it. He doesn't love it less; in fact, he's likely to love it more just because of this. The car is historic, because it is part of the current of time, and it is also now part of the restorer's personal history. It's started to become far more than a fact—it has stories associated with it; it has attained a status that is mythic.

Of course, there may be other currents at work, including making money on an "investment," but behind it all, there is a reason that people choose to pay high prices for what are impractical museum pieces. In an age when something new and improved appears every day, restoration of this sort—the honoring of the past—can be an eloquent statement about the longing for enduring values. And we must remember that other people do very similar things to their cars, even if they are not classics. They give them names, talk to them, love them, or even loathe them; or they decorate them at Christmas and place cuddly toys in them. They personalize them in endless ways.

To give another example, Harley Davidson riders spend a huge amount of money personalizing and accessorizing their motorcycles. This is not about going fast; Harley Davidsons are not noted for speed. What we are witnessing is a whole cloud of myths about who Harley Davidson riders perceive themselves to be, if they wish to live in that dimension. These myths are energetically fostered by the manufacturers and make a huge amount of money for them. Men and women buy and ride such motorcycles because they feel themselves to be different—feel better in themselves, in some ways, when they ride their machines. They have bought into a ritual activity that expresses a mythic idea, and at the end of the day they can shed it and go back to being lawyers or accountants if they wish. Harley Davidson has managed to key into what marketing guru and researcher Clotaire Rapaille calls a "cultural code," an unconscious language so deep and so powerful that many of us respond to it without quite knowing what it is.

The point to remember about these motorcyclists is that the mythic dimension they are buying into is, in many respects, one that has been fostered by astute money-making enterprises, and that the process is merely flattering to their egos. It does not necessarily give them a visceral connection to something spiritual, a sense of being more than themselves.

So, what is going on here? I suspect these psychic processes involved are exactly the same for modern man as they were for early man; it is the focus that has changed. We start finding burial goods alongside burials about 120,000 years ago, which indicates a personalized relationship between the individual and the object, one that is part of the story of who the individual was.[1]

In terms of evolutionary development, 120,000 years is nothing at all, so we can begin to make some connections across the millennia. The mythic way of seeing the world is essentially natural, and it is rooted in love, in real reverence for and attachment to the world that is observed around the individual. Whether it's a car or a flint-tipped spear, it gains value as a ritual object, or totem, in exactly the same way. The difference is that for early man all the parts of the landscape were mythic, and some were especially valued for personal myths. Thinking in this way connected our forebears to the land. Today it is, mostly, the personal possession that is mythologized, and often as a way of saying how important the owner is. What a loss of connection to nature and the eternal that reflects!

Myths of Food Gathering and Hunting

Most early myths—those that we know about, that is—are centered around the business of finding and creating food, for obviously this was a matter of enormous importance. In each instance, the myths have to do with wonder and gratitude. The plant that is destroyed when turned into food does not disappear forever but grows again next year, willingly giving itself up to be consumed again. The deer that is killed as part of the hunt is seen as giving its body for food. The hunter treats it with respect, so that successive generations of deer will be just as willing to provide for the group.

Again, the important aspects are that the animal or plant is treated with respect, even reverence, and is seen as part of the abundance of the earth. This is a process that is very different from walking into a supermarket and pulling a box of frozen hamburger off a shelf. Wonder, reverence, and love are what the mythic way of seeing can give back to us.

Here is Leslie Marmon Silko's description of a Native American deer hunt, which shows precisely this regard for the freshly killed animal:

> They sprinkled the cornmeal on the nose and fed the deer's spirit.
> They had to show their love and respect, their appreciation; otherwise, the deer would be offended, and they would not come to
> die for them the following year.[2]

If we visit the prehistoric caves of Lascaux or Altamira, with those heart-stopping depictions of animals painted on the rocks, it's clear that whatever those cave paintings were for such carefully observed figures and such precise details reflect a sense of wonder, even reverence. All those animals—the bulls, the bison, the horses, the antelope—would have been dangerous quarry, beautiful, fast, clever, and ultimately plentiful. The cave paintings seem to ask the basic question: How do we understand this wonderful place, our world? And it seems to give us back an answer of sorts: Perhaps we can't understand it; perhaps we can only experience it and be grateful.

The power of myth is not that it can be dissected and understood, necessarily; it is that it can be felt, and so it can connect us to a larger awareness of the world we walk on.

If you go into any of the great European cathedrals, perhaps around dusk, you do not have to know all the doctrinal details of the religions they uphold to get a sense of what the place is all about. You will *feel* that the place is holy. Walk around Stonehenge or Ankor Wat or the Buddhist caves at Ellora and Ajanta and, no matter what your beliefs or lack of beliefs, you will feel that others have been there who did certainly feel the holiness of the place.

Bullfighting as a Blood Ritual

The sense of a mythic landscape can also be preserved in strange and unusual ways. There is, for example, the "sport" of bullfighting, which is a national institution in Spain and in large parts of Latin America. It has recently been banned in the province of Catalonia, but the wonder is that this activity has survived so long, since the Spanish are not noticeably more cruel than any other culture. They feel passionately about their bullfighting, too. So how can we understand this?

The origins of bullfighting are cloudy, but we can see right away that this is a drama in which human intelligence and planning are used to subdue a very large and dangerous animal and turn it into food. It is therefore a demonstration of brain over brawn. We know from the frescoes in the Hall of Bulls at the palace of Knossos in Crete, which are more than 3,000 years old, that acrobatic displays involving men and women vaulting over charging bulls were important parts of religious ceremonies.

These magnificent frescoes seem to celebrate the triumph of mind over muscle. A long tradition of bullfighting in which the bull is not killed seems to be a direct result of this, ranging from Provence in France to Tamil Nadu in India, even to Japan. In fact, it seems likely that bullfighting in one form or another is an ancient way of demonstrating that cooperation, skill, and cunning can bring down or outwit even the largest foe. So the entire procedure can be seen as emphasizing community working together when faced with danger. This isn't a slight thing. To be able to demonstrate mastery over the largest and most frightening creature around at the time, in a world that was far less stable than ours, must have been profoundly reassuring.

One of the features of modern bullfighting, which we can presume to have been present for a long time, is that the bull is fought to the point of exhaustion. When it is so tired that it can hardly charge, the matador reverses the rhythm of the fight. He charges at the bull, this time on foot. With his sword he aims to drive the blade down the shoulder, through the ribs, and directly through the bull's heart, killing it cleanly. The clean kill is highly prized. It is seen as a death worthy of a good bull. Notice that no matter what we think of this cruel sport, there is some courage and respect for the animal involved, which is seen as admitting defeat and, therefore, delivering himself up to execution. This is not very different from the myths of hunting societies, which see the quarry as willingly giving up its life.

It's a motif we find again and again. The ancient Greek sacrifice of cattle involved placing garlands of flowers on the oxen or heifers, and the sacrificial animals were fed with fine food before the slaughter, to which each was led as a revered guest. They even had songs sung to them on their ways to the sacrifice. The revered sacrifice, willingly offering itself for the common good, will reappear much later as Jesus. There's a direct connection to the wine that is blood and the bread that is flesh in the communion service.

What we are looking at in the Spanish bullfight is a very ancient and dramatic celebration of a victory over a force of nature, which is made to bend to man's will. As such, it's not just about the need to control the forces of nature but also a metaphor for the need to fight our own internal demons with courage and skill until they do our bidding. For when we face our demons, when we tame them by not running from them, then they nourish our souls with their strength. The man who has faced difficulties and made it through the other side is stronger as a result, and he is also more alert to the dangers of the world.

When the crowd at a bullfight yells "¡Ole!" they do so because the fighter has just executed a particularly graceful movement within inches of the bull's horns, and therefore this is a mark of virtuosity. Bullfighters have sometimes returned from the fight with their tight-fitting clothes showing rips caused where the horns just snagged the material, and no more. But that cry of "¡Ole!" is, in fact, a corruption of the Arabic "Allah"—an acknowledgment that the skill of the fighter is god-given, a connection to something holy. The matador, in his traditional, stylized *traje de luz*, his "suit of light," is perceived as more than a mere mortal at such moments.

I don't care for bullfighting myself. I think it is cruel. Yet cruelty is only part of the issue since, for the watcher, it can articulate something that can barely be understood in simple terms. Every move made by the matador is a statement about facing life with skill and courage. Taking that spectacle away from some people, through the exercise of law, without giving them a ceremony to replace it, will lead only one way—to illegal bullfights in out-of-the-way places.

This is what happened with bare-knuckle "prize fighting"—which was energetically suppressed in 19th-century England but enthusiastically followed by crowds of thousands, even so. Boxing and other such sports are still with us today, so we know that banning these actions does not, and cannot, work. The reason it doesn't work is not because men are cruel and bloodthirsty, but because the actions in the ring speak of courage and skill and determination. If we focus on the blood we miss the meaning, which is visceral. We externalize our internal struggles by acting them out in the larger world. We all have difficult lives at times. We've all felt angry and wanted to lash out. So along comes an activity that becomes a ritual that expresses that feeling for us.

Banning such sports may, in the end, make about as much sense as cutting off the hand of a thief who steals a loaf of bread. It sends a message, but by focusing on the loaf of bread it ignores the hunger that drove the thief onward. What we're looking at here is spiritual hunger that is seeking expression.

At its most profound level, every activity in which there is a blood sacrifice, such as a bull, is a reflection of human sacrifice. In the north of Europe in pre-Roman times, and well into the early centuries after Jesus, we have evidence of human sacrifices in which young men or women were treated like kings and queens until they were led out to the holy rivers and killed.

The evidence of these sacrifices, preserved in peat bogs across Ireland, England, and Scandinavia, is now in our museums. As many as 1,850 such corpses have been found, but not all of them are definitely sacrifices. On occasions the well-preserved corpses have been excavated with the remnants of what appear to have been ritual meals still in their bellies, perhaps indicating that these were fertility sacrifices. Tollund Man, as he is now known, is almost certainly a ritual sacrifice of this kind. In an age when corpses would have been cremated, he was carefully buried in a peat bog after being hanged. Lindow Man died from three or four simultaneous wounds, echoing the "triple death" of Irish legends. His burial indicates special status, almost certainly as an offering to the gods.[3]

A full-grown bull, with his obvious sexual energy, is an appropriate and better sacrificial substitute than a young man or woman. Another substitute would be the bread and wine of communion, with its acceptance of, and transcendence from, the actual physical sacrifice. V. S. Naipaul records in *India: A Wounded Civilization* (HarperCollins, 1977) how he always wondered about the Hindu ritual of only men being allowed to cut into pumpkins, until he realized that the pumpkin was a substitute for the ancient pre-Hindu living sacrifices.[4]

To return to bullfighting, the important point to stress again is that this "sport," and others like it, is not really a sport at all; it's a ritual. The odds are so heavily stacked against the bull that this is a sacrifice, thinly concealed. Even hunting is more like a "sport" since the hunter never knows if he will shoot an animal, let alone know exactly which one. In almost every other sport the outcome is in question—which is why there is so much betting on the result. Those activities are truly open-ended, since we cannot be sure how the game will go and we cannot guarantee which side will win. This is why we have to treat events such as bullfighting as ritual events; they have nothing to do with "sport."

Bloodless Rituals of Violence

If we want a more accessible equivalent on our own doorsteps we could look at modern commercial wrestling, with all its odd derivatives. Here the spectacle is designed to be exactly that—a spectacle complete with wild and extravagant costumes, capes, even fireworks. The wrestlers engage in an elaborate and carefully choreographed struggle, some part of which is, most surely, staged. There are no quick endings such as one sometimes sees in professional boxing matches, where the fight can last 15 rounds or be all over in two minutes. In wrestling, the spectacle is spun out into a drama.

The overly dramatic gestures of the wrestlers are obvious to everyone. The man pinned to the floor, slapping his hand helplessly against the canvas, is signaling to us that this is difficult and painful. Yet, seconds later he throws off his assailant, and makes a spirited come back—the underdog no more, all pain forgotten, he hurls his opponent against the ropes and uses the forehand smash to render him (or some-times her) seemingly senseless. The crowds love it, and they love it in spite of its artificial quality.

In many cases, what we are looking at in wrestling is a dance in which a fight of good versus evil is acted out in exaggerated forms. Often the wrestlers enter the ring dressed in such ways as will instruct the audience as to who the hero is meant to be. During the Iraq war, a particularly popular wrestler was called "Sgt. Slaughter," complete with stars and stripes cape, and his opponent on at least one occasion was "The Iron Sheik." It was never in any doubt who was going to win; the question was merely how long it would take and what troubles would be involved.

Predictably, The Sheik was seen to cheat when the referee's back was turned, by delivering punches after the bell had rung, and so on. The referee pretended to be oblivious. This tended to drive the audience into a frenzy, as did the nasty smirks to the audience when The Sheik did something particularly unpleasant to his rival, whom he had unfairly tripped, or felled, in one case from outside the ropes. None of this was "seen" by the referee, of course…

Is this at all different from the predictable struggles of cartoon characters? How is this different from Tom and Jerry, or Elmer Fudd and Bugs Bunny, or comic book heroes? The premise is exactly the same. The purpose of such displays is that the "right" side wins, while taking the audience through certain emotional states. Sgt. Slaughter wins, as the audience wants him to, and in the process the audience gets to shout and rage and externalize all those feelings that they are not allowed to show at other times in the "civilized" world.

Wrestlers themselves are eager to point out that what they are doing is a type of acting, rather than an open-ended contest. John Cena, the 2010 World Wrestling Entertainment (WWE) champion, was recently interviewed about his move into a high-paying acting career. His comments, reported in Britain's *Guardian* newspaper, about the link between wrestling and theater are worth considering. Cena is entirely open about wrestling as entertainment. In fact, he says that movie acting is the same type of activity as wrestling. "It's really an extension of what we do. It's just in a different form. There's a ton of similarities." [5]

The movies that tend to be produced and marketed with wrestlers in main roles are predictably action packed and full of explosions of one sort or another. And the good guys usually win. Given Cena's words, it's fair, therefore, to look at wrestling as a spectacle that asserts a specific world order rather than, say, delving into human character traits. It's a special type of ritual, done for profit.

This ritual's value is that it reasserts a moral order, validates certain strong feelings, and seems to reward fair play and good, honest effort. It enshrines a particular version of courage. That's a pretty impressive array of achievements. It also delivers a rattling good spectacle, as far as many people are concerned. The audiences for wrestling matches such as these are an odd mixture, also. Scan the crowds and you'll see they are made up mostly of people under the age of 14 and over the age of 60. These may well be some of the least empowered members of our society, seeking some reassurance.

Video games have some of the same properties. The more violent games offer the player a chance to do violent things, but in a very specific way. Even though the player can be eliminated or "killed," in this sort of game the situation has been stacked in his or her favor right from the start because the developer wants everyone to have a good time. Yet it is a peculiarly sanitized world. You can get "killed" without feeling pain or terror. You can kill opponents without ever having to see their mutilated and suffering bodies up close, looking into their helpless and perhaps bitter gaze as life ebbs from them.

Talk to any soldier who has actually served in a real theater of war and you'll quickly realize that war games designed for entertainment purposes are highly stylized to protect the player. The agony of seeing your friends and buddies killed in front of your eyes, for example, is removed. Innocent civilian deaths, the mess and upset of war, hunger, thirst, fatigue—all these tend to be absent or played down. Yet anyone who has been in a firefight for even a few minutes knows how suddenly hard it is to breathe, how the heart races, how the limbs move more slowly than one would wish, and so on.

Such games offer sanitized war. Unfortunately, they often lead to people embracing war as a policy, or even as a career choice. If we go back to Aristotle, he suggested that drama should evoke pity and terror in the audience. The sense of pity was to come from our identification with the suffering character on the stage, and terror would be the natural response to seeing their difficult circumstances. That kind of drama was constructed specifically to alert us to human fragility, and to the courage needed to face that sort of challenge. It asks us to mobilize our courage and sense of purpose even though life is painful. That, really is the nature of courage—resilience attained even though the circumstances may frighten us.

I think you can see the differences. The video game does not deal with empathy, or with real courage, although it may evoke anger. The bullfight, although rigged in favor of human beings, does involve real courage; the wrestling matches we see on TV are also rigged, but they are closer to mere pantomime, often with a racist or a political agenda.

It's an important difference. Whenever we attempt to decode ritualized behaviors we gain experience in seeing exactly what is going on around us. Ritual and myth can be used to nurture many things and many attitudes. We need to be very careful which ones we choose to develop. Sometimes those that seem unpalatable at first may actually have a more vital message.

CHAPTER NINE

The Palio di Siena:
A Ritual of Social Competition

Let's now take a look at a different kind of ritual, one based in Siena, Italy. The Palio is a time-honored activity, a bareback horse race around the city *piazza* in Siena, and it has been going on in one form or another since at least the medieval period, finally finding its present form in 1590. Twice a year, in July and August, 10 representatives of the city districts, the *Contrade*, each select a horse and rider to compete in this wild race. The city streets are covered in earth, the masonry corners of the houses are padded with special mattresses, and an enormous crowd crams into the center of the main square to watch. The race can be won by a horse even without its rider, and as a special twist, the horse that comes in second is deemed to have placed dead last. There's no reward for playing safe, in other words. It's a recipe for a violent race, and during the three laps of the piazza, which take perhaps a total of 90 seconds, riders can be seen kicking and throwing punches at other riders, urging their horses to collide with the opposition, and taking every risk. The winner takes possession for one year of a *palio*, a cloth banner that is sacred to the Virgin Mary. There are two slightly different banners—one for each race.

This event is a major tourist attraction, but it also elicits ferocious dedication in the members of the various city *Contrade*. The entire occasion is an excuse for a gorgeous pageant of costumed drummers and flag twirlers, moving in procession, for several hours before the race itself, which usually takes place at dusk.

What seems fairly clear is that this race is all about the sublimation of group and tribal rivalries that would otherwise break out into open violence and vendetta. Each *Contrada* is like a tribe—a clan united in its own section of the city, with its own flag displaying an animal or mythic beast. The race is one way of having these potentially violent neighbors come into relatively friendly rivalry, so that on each occasion one or other gets to be the best, for a short while, with all the bragging rights attendant on that victory. It is a ceremony that honors the close-knit family structures while also insisting that these families have to learn to get on with each other the rest of the time. It is a warlike ritual of peace.

Now, we can imagine that in the 16th century the rulers of Siena must have been deeply troubled by these quarrelsome clans and their murderous rivalries. They might have thought that any such horse race would simply inflame more passionate party feelings and make things worse. Perhaps there were proposals to ban the races and lock up the troublemakers. There's logic to that way of thinking, but it would not have worked. The answer was, as we have seen, to incorporate the rivalry into the accepted life of the city, to allow it respect and space. The ritual of the Palio, therefore, both respects the psychological tensions and restrains them from their possible worse excesses.

Most of the world, Europe especially, knows about this in various other guises. Local soccer, rugby, and cricket teams have long been a way of a neighborhood asserting its collective identity, expressing its competitiveness and rivalry, and learning—inevitably—that the rivals have good qualities, too. It is, in fact, an essential ritual of independence and cooperation.

What's different about the Palio, though, is its specifically religious aspect. The victor's triumph has to do with winning the Palio for the local church, and involves both triumph at what one's team has done and humility for the Virgin Mary having made it happen. It represents, then, a template for living. We are expected to do our best, to work as hard as we can in our lives but, even so, we are not to expect success every time. In fact, the odds against winning are rather high. In a bullfight we know who will win; in a soccer match we know one side or the other will carry the day. In a horse race like the Palio it could be anyone's win. That's quite a subtle message.

It's not the same message that schoolchildren in most of the United States receive, which is that hard work and good grades definitely will pay off, and rewards will naturally come to you. The message created by the Siena Palio is less blandly reassuring. And perhaps its very realism is what makes it superior.

As we grow up we discover that many people work long and hard and do not get ahead at all. This can be acutely depressing to Americans, not because failure means starvation and death (it's really hard to starve to death in the United States) but because the illusion that we were all fed at school turns out to have been so cruelly unhelpful. Using the American line of thinking, we only have ourselves to blame for our "failure" to become wealthy. The American myth is, in contrast, less healthy than the message conveyed by the Palio.

The point seems to be this: People need and want local heroes; they want those heroes to win; but a champion who always wins merely breeds complacency and arrogance on one side and resentment on the other. A ritual like the Siena Palio gives us what we want, leaving aside the worst of the negative aspects. It gives us the drug we crave as well as the antidote. In this sense it is a social ritual, yet it also has a personal aspect. The ritual presents heroic actions that may or may not pay off as worldly success, but are praiseworthy even if they don't. This is not the fantasy world of Superman and action figure heroes who never lose. It's a world view we can actually live by.

CHAPTER TEN

Dangerous Myths:
Gun Ownership and War

Gun ownership is a phenomenon that is most strongly present in the United States, which allows almost all its citizens to possess a variety of weapons without very much formal regulation. In Europe and most of the rest of the world gun ownership is strictly controlled—or at least the authorities try to enforce that control. The exceptions, of course, tend to be in lawless parts of the world, like the hills of Afghanistan, Pakistan, and so on.

Many gun owners in the United States use their weapons for target practice or hunting. This is a right enshrined in the Constitution and to many it is an important aspect of being American. There's no point in questioning why it makes sense to spend hundreds of dollars and thousands of hours pursuing creatures that you may not particularly want to eat. For many gun owners, having a gun is the essence of being American, independent and free, and if that means being in possession of a powerful instrument that *could* take a life, even if you have no desire to do so at that specific moment, then that is part of the deal. And yet, could we not, perhaps, feel free and independent without actually owning a gun at all? I suggest we could, although that would require an inward process of building one's confidence. Buying a gun is easier.

I don't like the proliferation of guns on our streets, but I do recognize that for many people gun ownership is based on an inner drive that finds expression in this way, since it cannot find any other expression so easily. That is one reason that gun owners are not open to "reasonable" discussion—this is not about reason; it's about emotion. The less powerful we feel in our world, the more likely we are to want to purchase objects that confer power and prestige. Guns have become, for some of us, totemic objects with which we seek to console ourselves, since we have so few opportunities to exercise real courage. In this fascination with gun ownership, I think we can see a ritual that has gone astray.

In raising these issues it is not my intention to criticize anyone's culturally cherished values, or to point the finger of blame. I merely use this as an example of how, in modern life, we are surrounded by examples of powerful ritual objects whose original significance we have largely forgotten. When this happens, we lose our ability to navigate in a world imbued with meaning, full of potential understanding of our own resilient, independent nature. When we focus on the object, on the gun, we miss the meaning of which it is a symbol. It's like talking about strawberry-flavored ice cream without ever having plucked a perfect fresh strawberry and eaten it.

Gun owners often come from an honorable background of many generations of hunting or military activity, where the gun is as much part of what is accepted as "normal" as cowboy boots might be in a slightly different circumstance. As we know, some people will wear their cowboy boots even if they do not actually ride horses, even if they spend all day in their pickup trucks in town, or at the office. The boots and the guns are totemic objects, beyond convenient questioning.

This leads us inevitably to the next part of the discussion.

War as Ritualized Behavior

One of the most powerful rituals in which we currently engage is the highly stylized way we think about warfare. The notions of patriotism and homeland and so on are surely so threadbare by now that most intelligent people will treat the ideas with some care, even with some skepticism. As Bruce Springsteen said at a concert some years back, "Blind faith in anything will get you killed." So why is it that, knowing as we do the horrendous damage war does to everything it touches, we still speak the language of glory and victory? It can only be that we are not involved in a process of thinking about reality, but rather a process in which the activity itself has to be mythologized so that we can face it.

This mythologizing is as old as humanity itself. As we have already observed, the rituals of the hunt were created to salve the feelings of guilt that our primitive ancestors seem to have had about the prey they killed. They preferred to see the animals as willingly offering themselves for our nourishment, as long as they were treated with respect and offered prayer and ceremonies.

This ritual killing was not confined to animals and the unfortunate lower orders. We also have some evidence that kings in ancient Ur, in Sumeria, as well as in China, voluntarily sacrificed themselves at the end of a set period of time, together with their attendants, so that the new ruler could come forward. In the jungle civilizations of the tropical Americas, human sacrifice practiced extensively as a way of paying back the earth for the gifts it had given, which had to be "killed" by harvesting and consumption. This ritualized slaughter of citizens practiced by certain civilizations was child's play, of course, compared with the wholesale devastation of the two world wars that took place in the early 20th century.

Yet the myth remains that war is necessary, good, honorable, and somehow beneficial. It isn't. War has far-reaching and often unexpected consequences for the countries that engage in it. For example, thanks to continuous wars since Napoleon's time, the people of France are now considerably shorter in stature than they were before these hostilities began. That's because powerful alpha males, those most likely to go to war, are taller in stature. Once they had been killed in battle, only shorter men were left to reproduce. It's hard to see that this is beneficial. At one time, generations ago, it may have been true that warfare of the limited tribal kind, circumscribed by the seasons and the need to gather the harvest in fall, may have had a ritual purpose. It may have been important as a way to face dangers, and therefore to nurture courage. Those days are long gone, yet the myth remains.

But war has one thing we must not underestimate: It serves to focus attention. As award-winning journalist Chris Hedges points out in his book *War*, it is an activity that gives us meaning, even if the form it takes is less than desirable.[1] When war is declared, we have to let go of petty concerns. We are thrown into a state of emergency. Snap decisions have to be made. All this gives those most closely involved a sense of meaning, and it galvanizes every other citizen into becoming part of the support framework.

Even those who opt out of the activities are affected by it. The usual effects are shortages, the need to be careful with resources, and so on. No one involved has any doubt as to their role—social and personal roles have been assigned by the emergency. When this drama is over, it is sometimes very hard to come back down to earth again. A poignant example of this in May 2010 was Michael Ware, the Australian correspondent for CNN, who had to stop work because of combat-induced post-traumatic stress disorder (PTSD). Hedges' book is full of examples of journalists who found that reporting in a war zone was the most compelling thing in their lives—until some of them were killed. He cites several examples of those who were so profoundly engaged in the activity of reporting on the war, so immersed in it, that they sought out death—and found it.

When a state of war is declared life immediately changes, and it is almost impossible to maintain the usual pleasantries that soften everyday interactions. War is the ace of trumps that overturns our usual understandings about what matters and how we might want to explore our own inner riches. Certain discussions stop. If you're wondering about your survival, or that of your loved ones, it's hard to engage in other types of discussions, for instance.

War, it seems plain, is a force that upends all we understand. Now, some wars are fought for resources or to defeat oppression, but—and this is a big reservation—

most struggles for resources are not about shortages but about equitable allocation of those resources. Wars are more often fought because of some imagined threat to "our way of life" or "who we are." This is often felt most keenly by those who don't actually have a clear idea of who they are or what their way of life involves. These are the very people who respond most readily to vague rallying cries such as "patriotism." And so the discussion becomes confused.

In real terms, war is never worth it. In his book, Chris Hedges cites studies showing that after 60 days in a war zone, 100 percent of those involved show signs of psychological collapse. Put that in context by considering that currently a deployment to Iraq usually lasts a year. These damaged souls then return to their families (if they're lucky) and inflict at least some of this damage on spouses, children, and relatives. War is not a fire through which we pass, and which refines us in the process; it's not a poison that kills only the person who tastes it, either—it's an infection that spreads.

So why is this myth about the glory of war still so strong? One reason could be that we have no similar counterbalancing myth to keep it in check. Wars are sometimes inevitable, even necessary; but if we had a different myth—one that gave us another option we could invest in as heavily as we currently invest in war—then we might find a way of reversing the trend.

The rule of law, the perception of justice being served, could be just such a ritual. But the present legal system does not seem to be, in the public's eye, anything of the sort. We tend to see the rule of law as synonymous with "punishment" (which may help to explain why so many people want prisoners to suffer under very harsh conditions that have nothing to do with rehabilitation). Yet the very trappings of the law seem to show us another way forward. In court, the lawyers dress and talk in a particular way, never allowing the debate to become personally acrimonious. This is one reason why it is referred to as "the Law," rather than "what feels subjectively right or wrong." Judges at the international tribunal in The Hague wear long dark gowns and strange hats, all to signify that they are there as representatives of a higher order, not simply of their own interests. They could just as easily be priests in a temple.

Let's stand back from this discussion for a moment and think of it historically. When laws first make their appearance in our culture they are, above all else, instructions that are designed to avoid conflicts. In the Bible, the Ten Commandments constitute things we are expected to do or required not to do, in order to make sure that society remains relatively stable. If I don't covet my neighbor's goods or his wife, then I'm less likely to run into trouble. If I don't kill, then I won't spark a vendetta against me. Unfortunately, within a few pages of their appearance in the Book of Exodus in the Old Testament, the Ten Commandments seem to be forgotten because wars need to be fought and the Israelites need to fight them. The one set of events is a mute criticism of the other.

How can we reconcile these two extremes?

The implication is this: The world is horrible. It is full of disasters and tragedies and wars of unparalleled ghastliness. The challenge lies not in changing the world—which can't be done in short order—but in trying to teach ourselves how to live in it, poised between War and Law. The Bible stories tell us that we are creatures who tend to head toward war far more willingly than toward legal, civil processes. This illustrates our own nature to us but asks us to put that information into a context. It may be hard to see this but the Bible is full of such ritual stories—stories that tell us as much about ourselves as about the past… if we're paying attention. Such knowledge, even if it is bitter, frees us. That's when we can see the glories that are all around us, the beauties and the richness of life. What we need to do is acknowledge this central paradox and live with it.

Misunderstood Symbols

With this in mind, we can see other, basic icons of Christianity are available for us to use, if we can free ourselves from the orthodoxy of their religious overlay. Walk into any church. There are poignant symbols aplenty, if we can train ourselves to feel their significance, rather than taking them literally. When we see the image of Jesus crucified, for example, it ought to be deeply repugnant in the same way that any image of a tortured fellow human being would be. That a good, kind, godly, miracle-working, and generous person was treated this way is horrifying. But that is the way the world seems to work. The miracle is that, despite this, good people still come forward all the time. All too often, though, we have an intellectual understanding of the religious doctrine but don't feel the emotion behind it. When that happens we have a situation very like the one I included at the start of this book, when I described my own Confirmation ceremony.

But if we can revitalize the crucifixion by feeling its meaning, it becomes a living message, not a piece of doctrine that has to be explained away as "God becoming Man," or not becoming Man, with all the attendant wrangles of 2,000 years of clerical reasoning. When our spirit is crying out for meaning, it isn't really useful to get into intellectual discussions about whether Jesus could have avoided his own crucifixion since he was God the Son and, presumably, could have rewritten the situation. What matters is whether we feel human pity and sorrow for what Jesus endured, then allow that feeling to connect us to what it means to be alive in the world now. Jesus on the cross is an image of all that is best (his kindness), and all that is worst (the cruelty of man to man), about being on this earth.

That's when a tired religious image can be revitalized and connect us to a larger myth about what a "good life" might mean.

In the same vein, when we view an image of the Madonna and Child, it's merely a distraction to speculate on the reality of Virgin Birth, or whether the Virgin Mary was still a virgin after giving birth to Jesus. The Catholic Church argues strongly that she was; but we would do better to look at the image itself, a mother and her child, and remember that this is a depiction of deep love and unconditional acceptance—something that will become less available to the child as he grows older. It's an image of the holiness of the Creator's love for the things that are created, because a mother's love for her child is exactly that. In choosing to empathize with the unconditional love between mother and child, we may find ourselves understanding the power of God, or whatever we call our higher power. It doesn't matter what religion we normally belong to, or even if we don't identify ourselves as religious, we can feel it if we let ourselves be human.

We have plenty of images to help us; we just don't feel their power, and consequently don't use them effectively. There's nothing wrong with the images themselves. What's wrong is that, like an old picture in a museum that has been varnished one too many times, we simply can't see the images clearly any more. All we can see is the dark, crackled surface.

Nonetheless, images such as these could be used to steer us away from the fascination with war and killing, which seems to be one of the salient features of our culture. These traditional images offer us a view of what is best in a difficult world, and we could choose to prize those values more than warfare. If we could do that, we could move toward a different state of mind—one that promotes peace and honors the sanctity of life. This might be one antidote to the myth of war. Another might be found in the mythology of the Law, if we could revalue it.

Again, with our current image of the law, we tend to associate all things legal with a slow, painfully tedious process, great expense, and ultimately a disappointing outcome. It's a trade that makes lawyers rich but doesn't garner them much real respect in the public eye. What a pity. If we chose to respond differently, we could see the law as being graced with patience, skillful thought, the desire to winnow truth from falsehood, and the wish to reward those who are good (and not just to punish those who have erred). We could choose to see it that way. We could see it as an elegant expression of civic management. And yet we don't.

This brings us back to where we started—that war, or drama of any sort, gives us a sense of meaning in our lives. It gives us the illusion of being fully present, now. It succeeds in this by keeping the intellect engaged and giving that restless part of the brain something to chew on. This is a bit like diverting a dog from chewing your chair leg by giving it a bone—it is a substitute activity. Could we imagine, instead, a way of living that includes a healthy respect for not getting busy? Could we envision being able to be at peace with simply being, rather than having to do things all the time?

For many of us, that idea often takes the form of a vacation at the beach, where we stop doing what we usually do and just relax into doing nothing. The slight disadvantage of this is that the solution is as extreme as the activity that has become a problem. Two weeks in the Bahamas feel good because they're a change from our usual life. But while we're sitting in the sun, we are always making the comparison implicitly: this is vacation; that is how I make money.

The better way forward is to try and release ourselves from making any comparisons, so that we can relish being in the place of simple existence—a goal that is deceptively demanding in its simplicity: less is more.

Joseph Campbell offers an exquisite example of this in his story about the young warrior in Japan being trained to be a fighter, and I am going to use it here for a slightly different purpose.

For the first couple of years the trainee swordsman doesn't even touch a weapon. He sweeps and fetches water and tidies up after the more senior trainees. During this time the master will, at unexpected times, pop up and whack him with a cane. The trainee doesn't know when the next attack will come, or from what direction. So he starts to hone his alertness skills. Will the attack come from over there? Or from behind him? Or somewhere else? What the trainee quickly learns is that by focusing on the possibility of an attack from a specific direction he blanks out awareness of all the other directions, thereby making himself vulnerable. He learns to become fully aware of all directions at the same time, equally, and to remain in this place of full awareness and centeredness.

It's an elegant way of describing the mental discipline of being as aware, as present, as possible. The trainee still has to go about his daily tasks, just as we all do. The chores have to be done. But the important thing is to be fully aware of being in the present moment without judging or preconception. This is when we can free ourselves from the web of thought that says things must be one way, from the web of conventional thinking. Life, at the level of open awareness, is not about planning; it just happens. It unfolds as it has to.

As with many Oriental trainings, it's about more than just getting a specific level of expertise. It is about a philosophy that can take us to the highest levels. It is, perhaps, about passionate caring and passionate not caring at the same time. Ultimately it's about contacting a sense of peace through being alert, through being present.

If we were to train our awareness in such a way it could be used to counterbalance our culture's most weighty myths: war, getting ahead, "winning," and dramatic action. For if we are free of conventional thinking we can experience things with more directness. Before the intellect came into our lives, before the longings of ego began to make themselves felt to drive us to desire those material things we think we want, there was another experience. Many people tend to think of this in dismissive terms, as being similar to what the young child has to grow out of in order to "mature." I'd like to suggest that we need to mature but we may also wish to retain the sense of undifferentiated being that links us to all things. We needn't throw out the earlier awareness just because something else has come long.

And if we truly feel linked to all things through this undifferentiated awareness, then how could there be any war? Fighting another person would be merely fighting oneself.

The novel *The Golden Compass,* by Philip Pullman, provides a charming example of this state of readiness. One of the characters in the book is a huge polar bear, a *panserbjorn,* called Iorek Byrnison. His great talent is that he will never flinch if someone pretends to aim a blow at him, but the moment the blow is intended to hurt he can, quicker than lightning, block it. No one knows how he does it, and neither does he. He just knows. He's a formidable friend and a ferocious enemy.

Iorek Byrnison's story is that he has been cheated out of his rightful place as head of the terrifying Bear Clan. He wants only one thing: to be who he was meant to be and has been blocked from becoming. He helps the characters he interacts with because they have promised to free him from his enslavement, which came about through his own doing when he was drunk. In some ways Pullman's character is a version of what we are talking about with the Japanese trainee warrior, since the polar bear is totally aware of what is going on around him, yet knows that he has allowed himself to be enslaved and forced to work at menial jobs.

Pullman's book is a moral fable of some subtlety. It explores the ways that organizations seek to control minds—specifically, children's minds—so it is not to be disregarded lightly. It is exactly the topic we are considering here, and the questions Pullman asks about the human psyche are fascinating. If war is an activity that offers us the illusion of purposefulness and focus, then could we not hope for that sense of purpose and focus without buying into the illusion? We know from the Japanese example that those mental abilities can be developed. Is that the only way to develop them? Clearly, there are other ways. Meditation is one. Unfortunately, meditation is not easy, nor is it possible to impose it upon entire populations. Yet perhaps it may be a way forward.

Perhaps the two examples serve us in another way. Animals, Pullman suggests, can achieve this state of awareness naturally. It doesn't make them better than us, merely different and troubled by different things. Iorek is hardly a happy or fulfilled polar bear, and he has plenty of basic ego drive. But his desire is not to wage war and hurt others en masse; it is to fight the one creature who cheated him—his rival. And he wants to kill him, plain and simple. In this novel, it is the human beings who want to force others to think their way, manipulate them, while creatures like Iorek are merely being true to their nature.

Pullman's view is helpful, then, since his novel depicts the central human weakness that leads us toward making aggression and war into mythic experiences: the desire to possess whatever it is that animals naturally possess—that sense of being fully present. We think we can only do this by creating a drama, however. Perhaps that's why George Orwell, in *1984*, envisages a world in which there is a perpetual war of some sort going on. In that world, warfare really is a form of "peace," since agreeing to the war means people can stop thinking about anything else, so, paradoxically, they can be "at peace" with the situation.

All forms of human behavior have their associated rewards; that's why we continue to do them. Sometimes they are not the best reward. We scratch an insect bite, and it simply itches more. But for the moment we are scratching, it feels so much better. The desire for war seems to be one of those actions that is understandable but not, as it happens, healthy. Our challenge is to dismantle, or replace, the structures of ritual and myth that have kept this notion so strong, despite everything.

CHAPTER ELEVEN

Ritual Occasions That Have Changed Their Emphasis:

Childbirth

Pregnancy and childbirth are facts of life, and in most societies they are seen as moments of profound change to be honored and enjoyed. Ask anyone who has been present at the birth of a child. Talk to the new father, for example, especially if this is his first child, and the chances are you'll see someone who is stuck for words, who has been moved, and startled, and perhaps frightened. Often he cannot convey his emotions in words. Yet if you've been there, beside him through the whole thing, you'll be bonded to him and his child in a way that you will always feel in your bones. There is a shared bond for the bystanders and, of course, there is a powerful bond between the parents, which is validated by the whole group.

Childbirth was not always like this. In fact, for our purposes, it is a truly excellent example, as the rituals surrounding it arose pretty much naturally out of existing circumstances in bygone times. As we know, in many societies childbirth was an event attended only by women; men were discouraged from attending. Presumably, the men were likely to be in the fields, or hunting, or elsewhere, and the only reliable help for the less than mobile mother-to-be was likely to be other women. So the midwife became a valued role, and childbirth became a women's activity, with certain local variations in custom that were upheld through the ages. It became a ritualized event.

In our present world, though, we are in danger of minimizing what could be a powerful chain of events in our culture. All too often, pregnant women go into labor and are taken to the hospital, where their babies are frequently delivered by caesarian section, and new mothers often wake up without their newborn nearby. Many, if not most, of the doctors are men. Relatives, even spouses, may be excluded. Framing the event this way has sent two powerful messages. One is that mothers cannot complete the childbirth process on their own because they are not competent. The second message is that this is a job for professionals, so move over!

Now, clearly I'm exaggerating here, but a few years ago this was exactly what was happening in American hospitals. Fathers and relatives were routinely kept out of the delivery room; now they are encouraged to be part of the process in many places, although usually only one person is allowed to attend. In the past, also, the baby was whisked away from the mother immediately after birth, only to be returned at a later time, cleaned and tidied.

This may have been very good at preventing infections and possibly even for saving lives, yet it was not always very good for families. Findings reported by The Colorado School of Energy Studies (CSES) and The Santa Barbara Graduate Institute show that this process interrupts the primal bonding that occurs when the newborn is placed at the mother's breast. While these findings are not universally accepted, the evidence strongly suggests that the action of having the child placed with the mother right after birth allows for the child's heartbeat to regularize. The baby, after all, has spent months hearing the mother's heart, and has felt in tune with that rhythm. Now, after birth, placing the child near the mother's heart allows the familiar heartbeat to be heard and sensed in a new way, reassuring but less loud.[1]

This way of thinking ties into what is now referred to as "The Kangaroo Care" principle, after the widely reported example of an Australian couple whose newborn was declared dead by doctors, but revived after being placed directly on the mother's breast.[2]

Babies also need this skin-to-skin contact, it seems, in order to regulate their nervous systems. John Chitty, RPP, BCST, one of the most respected professors at CSES, offers an example of a newborn twin giving a "rescuing hug" to the weaker twin, who was expected to die, but then revived after a nurse acted on an inspiration and placed them both in the same cot.[3] There is a growing body of such anecdotal evidence, which suggests that what once came naturally as part of the childbirth rituals was, in fact, extremely helpful to the child and the mother. Our modern birthing practices have a lot to answer for, even if the emphasis on hygiene and medical intervention when needed has saved many babies' lives.

Since these benefits for the child and mother are extremely hard to measure objectively, the medical establishment has been reluctant to accept them. So many variables come into play that many doctors claim it's almost impossible to tell if a child is "better" or "worse" off for the experience, so the rationalists of the medical world deny the evidence. Instead, they opt for a quick hygienic bath for the infant and separation from the mother.

Even when the whole childbirth experience is much more sensitively handled, there are still surprising deficits. For example, couples are encouraged to come to pre-birth classes, where they learn about what to expect, how to respond, what signs to look for, and so on. As a result many couples bond more closely with each other, and they also make friends and network with acquaintances, which will be useful in the months ahead. This is good.

And yet it is all, surely, only a relearning of what was always there in other, less developed societies. So let us imagine a pregnant woman in a rural community. From the start of her pregnancy she will have family and friends around her, offering advice (whether she needs it or not), discussing the arrangements, and helping to prepare for the child. With luck these will be competent and loving presences, although that can't always be guaranteed. As the due date approaches the mother will not feel alone because these people will be around her, watching, advising, and giving their opinions. The birth itself will be an event that is, fundamentally, a shared experience. Family members, the local midwife, the grandmother—all will have their roles to play and the newborn will be received into the family circle, literally into the arms of the family. The emotion of the event will be shared, above all. Several people may help to wash the baby and the mother, and all will have much to say about what they've all been through.

This may not look like a ritual, since it is a series of events spread over a very long period of time, yet it most certainly becomes a ritual. It conveys more than just getting the job done efficiently and safely; it is a shared experience, delivering a profound message about the power of family.

Today, in the West, with families spread all over the globe, the welcome message communicated by this older communal process can be lost totally. The opportunity to show families as essentially supportive and loving (even if there may be other tensions) does not always occur. So we are left only with the sense that families are far flung and estranged from one of the most moving experiences available to anyone.

The results of this changed approach to birth are hard to evaluate because (once again) there are so many variables. Yet we can venture to say that, on the whole, the child who is received into a family community is more likely to feel loved, secure, and that he or she has a "place" in that community. The mother will, also, tend to feel less alone. Obviously this is not always the case. But what could be more lonely than the woman in the Manhattan hospital bed, in a ward full of strangers, who has been attended by a friendly but professionally distant staff of doctors and nurses, and who now holds her baby for the first time, several hours after it has been born? Perhaps she has been sedated with an epidural and has been out cold through the delivery, and she now awakes, groggy and dazed. Perhaps she is alone as she waits for her husband, if she has one, knowing that her family are in Kansas, or Wyoming, or wherever. She'll have to tell them all about it, by phone or e-mail, one by one. It's a task she doesn't want or need at a time when she'll be exhausted from childcare. That is no substitute for a shared experience, and it's no substitute for the conversation of relatives as they gossip among themselves about what happened. The "village" event as I shall call it, offers more and more possibilities for social interaction, and thus for welcome of the new infant.

I don't think we can go back to the "village" way of life very easily in our mass culture, so it may seem to be merely nostalgic to even mention it. Even so, there are distinct aspects of social cohesion that get lost when a ritual occasion such as this becomes modernized. We may have healthier babies, but we may also produce more alienated and disaffected families, more breeding grounds for strife and aberrant behavior, where children are neglected, shoved out of the family, abandoned, or exploited.

Within the earlier structure, when the mother and child felt held and acknowledged by the family, there was a sense of lives being lived with more certainty, more courage. It meant there was less possibility of a confused, tired, and inexperienced mother second-guessing her own decisions, panicking, or assuming she needed expert help from outside.

Today, experts seem to be taking over in this realm, telling us how to raise our children. The over-prescription of drugs to children in the United States is widely recognized by educators. So many children are misdiagnosed with disorders, from attention deficit hyperactivity disorder (ADHD) to schizophrenia, that we must conclude that this is not the mark of a confident society that knows what to do with its children. It is the mark of bewildered parents, feeling alone, who prefer to trust drug companies and experts rather than notice that their own anxieties are being reflected back to them in the child's behavior. Since expert opinions change almost as rapidly as the fashions this is a dangerous way to proceed.

Rituals, especially family rituals, don't just enhance the moment and let us know what is to be cherished in life; they also show us what we, as humans, have to have in place in order to continue to be a stable society. Childbirth may now be more safe and hygienic than before, but it has in some cases achieved this by abandoning some important behaviors, social rituals that have been useful for generations before our own time. We must be careful that in our desire to do what is reasonable—whether during childbirth or at any other time—we do not carelessly dispose of some emotionally important actions that can strengthen the social bonds that sustain us.

CHAPTER TWELVE

Myth Is Everywhere —
If You Look For It

At this point it probably looks to you, the reader, as if almost anything can be made out to have a mythic or ritual structure. And that is precisely the point I'm trying to establish. We are part of a mythic structure that effectively encompasses everything—but our tendency is to deny that and place the ego needs first.

In ancient times, the entire landscape was mythic for the early people who lived in it. Ours is no less filled with meaning; it is simply that the meanings have become uncoupled from their source. Early societies had to work hard to find out what were the most useful mythologies to support their lives and their psychological needs. They did this by listening to their unconscious images, arising through dreams, trance, stories, and in many cases through what seemed to be "right"; and so mythologies developed.

Those societies that had poorly developed or incoherent mythologies would have been weaker, less able to define themselves or establish a sense of purpose, and would have died out. We know this to be true from modern circumstances.

For example, when the belief systems of American Indian societies are undermined by the incursions of a modern world of technology and change, they tend to disintegrate rapidly. Alcohol has decimated Indian tribes, many of whom are now confined to reservations, often a long way from their ancestral homelands, where they are divorced from their tribal understandings, traditional ways of life, and a sense of purpose.

American Indian reservations, particularly those located on the Plains, such as the Lakota Sioux Reservation in South Dakota, are a sad and desperate place for many tribal members. American Indian tribes were once highly efficient, coherent societies that had coexisted peacefully with their environment for a very long period of time. Deprived of their traditional ways of life (the wanton slaughter of the buffalo herds is but one example of the way the European invaders destroyed the lives of many

Indian tribes), dispossessed of their lands, many Plains Indians died in the late 1800s during the Indian Wars. Many of the survivors have yet to find any meaningful myth or ritual life to replace what they have lost. The result is often destructive and self-destructive behaviors that show all the hallmarks of a societal deathwish.

Yet there is hope. Novelist Leslie Marmon Silko, whom we have already mentioned, grew up on the Laguna Pueblo Reservation. She writes movingly about the ways we can realign ourselves with the land, the creatures on it, and the power of nature, in order to reclaim the soul. Her magnificent work *Ceremony*—first published more than 30 years ago—tells the tale of a traumatized World War Two veteran who is healed by the rituals of his tribe and of his unconscious, which help him reconnect with the land and the spiritual power of nature. It's a recurrent theme in Silko's writing, especially her most recent work, *The Turquoise Ledge: A Memoir*, in which she introduces the reader to the feeling of what it means to be fully, wondrously, connected to the world of nature. This is our challenge, too.

Let me give you an example of what I mean.

When I was a boy and later a young man in England, we had a general sense of what it meant to be English, and that's what we wanted to be. It wasn't so much a national pride as an awareness that "we" tended to understand things in certain ways, and not others. Now, visiting England 24 years later, it feels as if everyone wants to be American, because that's where the money and excitement is. Young English people feel less and less rooted or placed within a culture they can identify as vital.

This hasn't been helped by such social problems as unemployment and a poor economy, of course, where many people have found it almost impossible to find meaningful work. One reason I left England in 1986 was because I could feel what being underemployed, and even unemployed, was doing to my psyche. I needed a job that felt meaningful and was a good fit for my skills in order to maintain my sense of self as an effective human being. I needed to contribute to my society, and I couldn't find a way to do so. And I wasn't alone in this.

What I didn't fully realize when I left was that the landscape in which I had grown up, those rolling farmlands and beech copses, had already claimed a portion of my being. Leaving that landscape made sense in terms of a career, but it also cut me off from things I understood and people I knew at a deep level, because we had been shaped by the same landscape.

The economy had let us all down, but so had our cultural myths. My area of expertise at that time, English Literature, could be a powerful force in education for growing personal awareness, compassion, and examining the way lives are lived. I knew that. My peers knew it, too. But if you're hungry and cold, these values seem like a luxury rather than a necessity.

At the other end of the spectrum, people who are very wealthy in monetary terms feel they don't need social myths and understandings—they have money that gives them freedom from such considerations. As a result, in no time at all, they find themselves surrounded with wealth but not, alas, with meaning. The therapists' couches of the world are filled with wealthy neurotics looking for meaning and purposes they can believe in.

Attachment as a Refuge

In the West, we tend to look for "meaning" through our attachment to others, rather than to locations or to the spirit of the land. Romantic love is held as the highest achievement, the cure for all that ails you, and with that comes a subsequent emphasis on attachment to children. These small islands of familial love and hope are essential, of course, because they represent belonging in a mass culture where belonging to any unit larger than the immediate family now seems impossible. "Family values" is a phrase that has enormous power for many people, quite a few of whom have no families to speak of. It suggests a time when we knew where we stood, or so we imagine. We need myths, therefore, to help give us a structure that can show us what fulfillment is, and what it involves, and we don't have that any more.

Television offers some clues here, because of the values it seems to enshrine. The programs that run longest and are most beloved are those that seem to suggest social consistency. The sitcoms that are based on groups of people who routinely see each other (*Seinfeld, Friends, Sex in the City, Desperate Housewives, 90210, Melrose Place, Cheers, The Cosby Show*, and so on) all give us a sense of "family" and community that most people do not experience in their lives.

People can, of course, have fairly strong differences with members of their families and wrestle with these for years, feeling alienated and alone. Perhaps part of what makes daytime soaps so appealing is that they also show the same cast of characters working through their dramas over periods of years. What is important here is that all these people are passionately engaged with each others' lives. That's what makes the drama. For most of us, though, real life is likely to be filled with large numbers of people we see every day who are not even vaguely interested in our lives, nor are we that interested in theirs. The passionate engagement just isn't there.

Today, we cling to myths of family and social activities, when statistically people are lonelier and more likely to be unattached than ever before. The fact is that we are yearning for a series of myths quite at odds with reality. But if we are willing to take some time to examine them, the myths themselves tell us what we are lacking. We could then use that information to create our own updated version of community.

We know what we want and need; we just don't know how to create it. The reason is that we don't have strong ritual behaviors in position any more. Many of us don't know how to be part of a community, so we can't get the benefits of it. We are like mountain climbers who can see the summit—which here means the sense of being connected to others in a vital way—yet we don't have any equipment to help us scale the heights.

Community, family, and small organizations are all held together by small actions and behaviors that are recognized as good and kind. The coffee break, the shared baked goods, the donuts that seem to be in every office staff room—all these build a sense of belonging and so can be seen as rituals. But we need more than this. We need some sort of shared activity that asserts common moral values—the kind of shared activity that used to be supplied by the churches.

This is important. The mark of a successful myth is that it enables us to deal with our world in ways that allow us to feel effective. We do something, knowing that it is right and good and proper by the standards we have. We feel effective and secure. So, for example, we may raise and educate children in a particular way because this is "the way it's done." We can see if we're doing our part properly, and if there's a problem we have a way of addressing it.

The trouble starts when we are told that there are dozens of ways of raising and educating our youngsters, that no one's sure which one is the right one, and it doesn't matter that much anyway because the world is changing so fast we don't know what we're raising our children to become. We just want them to get good grades and go to a "good school," without much idea of what a good school actually is, or could be.

Now, I'm sure many people will read that, feel angry, and say that they work hard to make sure their kids are raised properly, and so on. And I have no doubt they do. From my years spent in education, I also have no doubt that many worthy and loving parents are confused, well meaning, and feel alienated from their children, whom they work so hard to support and nourish. Parents are doing the hard work of earning the money and being supportive, yet the larger society is not always able to guide our children effectively when they step outside the front door. Our social myths—depicted in those values we yearn for and that our TV shows revere—tell us what we need, but we're going to have to pay attention to that information and then work to create the structures that are necessary.

PART IV

We Need Myths,
But How Can We Choose
Productive Myths?

Some Practical Guidelines

"Ritual is the way you carry the presence of the sacred.
Ritual is the spark that must not go out"

—*CHRISTINA BALDWIN*

CHAPTER THIRTEEN

Bogus Myths and How To Identify Them

Before we can choose productive myths for our lives we must be sure to weed out the bogus myths first. Some of these will be very deeply rooted, and therefore harder to deal with.

One of the marks of a bogus myth is that it acts like carrot-and-stick persuasion. So, for example, if we take a look at some political myths, we'll see that the parties that uphold "freedom" often use that buzzword as a cover for something they are, in fact, taking away.

For instance, the Republican Party in the United States wants citizens to keep their guns, since everyone is entitled to hunt and protect themselves; yet, the party does not work to protect the jobs of so many of its poorest voters. We get to keep our guns but not our jobs, which are outsourced to other countries. We have our "freedom" but at a cost.

Similarly the Republican rhetoric around the health care debate was that we should be "free" to choose our health care, which means that the government should not help us to get health care since that would impact our freedom to choose. Now, this makes no sense. It's like saying to a starving person that since giving him food would be the equivalent to telling him how to run his life it's less coercive, and therefore healthier, to let him starve.

Again, the Republican Party has in recent times consistently campaigned against new taxes, and even fought to repeal existing taxes so we can keep more of our hard-earned dollars. At the same time, during the tenure of George W. Bush it deregulated Wall Street, thereby allowing certain people to rob most of us of our saved dollars and retirement funds without any recourse in law. They did this all in the name of "freedom." Now, I'm not just taking a cheap shot at a specific political party; I'm looking at this from the point of view of what the image might be that we're buying into when we accept such strange logic. When we see this series of contradictions, we might suspect a pseudo-myth has been created in order to manipulate us.

The purpose of a successful myth is to bring us into a place of greater acceptance of life's contradictions and problematic areas. An unsuccessful myth, a pseudo-myth, tends to leave us feeling angry and cheated instead. The Republican Party myth is just such a myth. It seems to preach that citizens who are angry are, therefore, empowered to make good decisions about their own welfare and take care of themselves better.

On the other side of the fence are myths that are just as questionable, associated with the Democratic Party. One of these myths is that providing assistance to the most vulnerable will eventually make our society "better." This is a fine and compassionate aim, but in practical terms it too often has the result of infantilizing those who are not capable, often at tremendous cost to society as a whole. If we are to support all those who need and deserve support, and do so adequately, then we'll face a considerable shortfall of resources very soon. The world's population is growing, and the world itself is straining to provide for us all. Sooner or later this myth, as presently constituted, will lose credibility.

The real situation is that we have a duty to help the unfortunate, educate and empower them, so that they do not become passive recipients of welfare and can once again be an active part of our society. It's eminently possible to do this, but it requires a massive infrastructure. It demands the care, love, and devotion of many citizens— and a humane point of view shared by all those who will pay for it. This is, I'm sure you'll admit, more than a simple "tax hike" to fund "vital services" can achieve on its own, which is the way it's presented to the electorate. This compassionate vision requires a whole other way of doing things, a totally different way of thinking about citizenship, money, and resources. Yet, all too often, the problem gets boiled down to an either-or political equation, where we view one party's myths as hopelessly flawed but not our own.

So we have to ask deeper questions about voters who cling to these, or any other, myths. In Republican mythology, the myth of guns and rugged individualism is translated in everyday terms into a desire for lower taxes and a line of thinking that states "Don't tell me which doctor I should choose." Such attitudes offer us important clues about a particular worldview, but when linked to the overwhelming evidence of an uncaring and callous government system, we see a strange picture. Here are voters who seem to welcome those who allow them be fiercely independent and who accept that the government will not take care of them when they need it. In their minds, this is a reasonable state of affairs.

The closest comparison I can make is with the Old Testament version of God in the Bible. Here is a God who has no hesitation in banishing Adam and Eve. They, in turn, accept their banishment as deserved punishment for their original sin, which will be passed onto their descendants forever. That doesn't seem fair to the descendants, somehow. This same God urges the Israelites to make savage and genocidal wars on their neighbors (which they do), and he punishes Job for no obvious reason. And this is the God who allows the Israelites to be enslaved in Egypt, then blasts the Egyptians with plagues and death, only to have the freed Israelites wander in the desert for decades.

It's hard not to see this version of God as arbitrary, angry, and terrifying. We could put this in some sort of context by comparing the Bible with the Hindu sacred text, *The Bhagavad Gita*. There we find plenty of advice about how to live in the world, how to cultivate one's inner awareness, and how to face the contradictions of the world. Even though *The Bhagavad Gita* opens with Arjuna facing a battle, it quickly becomes a philosophical discourse of some subtlety as Krishna puts him right on a few major points. It's an entirely different sort of text. There's plenty of spiritual and practical advice. We do not find much of this in the Old Testament, which at times seems more like a catalog of horrors than a guiding text. In their broadest terms both texts are about fighting, which is why it's helpful to compare and contrast them. But the Old Testament is not about doing anything other than following God's will in an oppositional world in which God's will is often arbitrary and usually about might making right.

The Democratic Party's general myth would seem to be closer to what we see in the New Testament, where the poor and disenfranchised are held to be more worthy than the rich. "The meek shall inherit the earth," we are told in the Sermon on the Mount, which spells it out for us. It's an attractive proposition, that the weakest and most vulnerable are worthy of full respect; yet, it's not hard to see how it could run into serious opposition from the Old Testament view. And, in fact, it did, since Jesus was crucified in what was clearly a pragmatic move by the Romans. Wishing to avoid a riot and perhaps many deaths, they elected instead to go with what seemed to be the popular mandate. This was sound politics and, ultimately, compassionate of human life in general.

We could see our political battles as ultimately irreconcilable: both myths are equally powerful and equally flawed, and both deliver disappointment. By the same token, if we want to create common ground, it's essential that we acknowledge the myths driving both parties. We cannot do that, though, if we reject one or other of the myths as flawed or evil or immoral. In fact, both myths are flawed, and it's time to see behind the charade. What will replace them is something we haven't even begun to look for yet, because we're too busy arguing.

In case this comparison seems too extreme for you, I'll back it up by pointing out that it has been a Republican party policy for some time now that the Ten Commandments (as laid down in the Old Testament of the Christian Bible) should be displayed in state senate houses, courthouses, and schools. These moves have been resisted by Democratic Party supporters, leading to the same sort of gridlock at the state level as we see in the U.S. Congress.

Whenever we come across this sort of stalemate we can be fairly sure that two myths are colliding. The trouble is that our reality seems to require us to believe different parts of both myths. We yearn for a world of peace and compassion and respect for all, in which we come to know our divine nature as creatures that are a part of the infinite universe. Yet we also wonder how we're ever going to pay for it. We're afraid that if we are peaceful then others will attack us. How can we balance these two aspects? It seems impossible.

If we change the terms of discussion, though, we may find a way forward. The real struggle for each and every one of us is not just against the outer world of threat but against the ways in which the ego can lead us to selfishness and mere materiality. We must seek, somehow, to live successfully in both worlds. We must be compassionate and decisive, and that is not easy.

Unfortunately, as it stands right now, we have no public myth we can tap into that can help us confront this situation—it is simply a grim fact of life, which people face with courage or desperation. Just like those little boys who went with me to boarding school all those years ago, we have no collective myth that allows us to view the present situation as anything other than a confrontation of political values. The lack of a guiding myth at this time in history prevents us from dealing with the very real and urgent problems we face. So, Global Warming and Climate Change are left under-addressed. The crisis of overpopulation is dealt with piecemeal, country by country, or not at all. And the list goes on.

CHAPTER FOURTEEN

What Do Myth and Ritual Supply?

So what is it we need from our myths? Joseph Campbell, the preeminent research-er of myth and legend, cites four aspects of myth that he deems essential:

- **Myth should awaken the "mystical function."**
  It should open up the individual to "awe and gratitude" for the wondrous thing that is our existence. Once that mystical function has been awakened, there is no such thing as a mere fact—facts are now seen as part of a dimen-sion of the universe that is mysterious and wonderful, and above all not to be feared.

- **The image of the universe that this mythology provides should be in tune with the scientific awareness and general knowledge of the world as we inhabit it**.
  Myth should be plausible, above all. If this doesn't happen, then we find ourselves with the sort of problems we see today, where some people choose to believe the creationist myths of the Bible and others feel they are absurd and out of phase with current thinking. What has happened is that an old myth has begun to wear out. As it does, so the important messages it holds for us no longer feel accessible.

- **Myth should validate the norms of the society that has adopted it.**
  Myth reinforces the reasons for a society to do the things it does in the way it does. Not all societies are the same. For example, Sharia Law, as practiced in some Islamic nations, may be completely consistent with the understand-ings of that society and entirely coherent in itself, yet to a western observer, it may seem barbaric. The stoning to death of women convicted of adultery, even when in some cases the adultery would be defined in the West as rape, seems bizarre to us. By the same token, the sexual freedoms allowed women

in the West may seem immoral in those places that practice Sharia Law. Each is operating under a different set of understandings, and each values different myths.

- **Myth can act as a guiding force for each person, preferably over the whole course of his or her life**.
  Because it fits in well with the overall social expectations of the society that embraces it, a society's myth can also be successfully applied to the individual life.

These four aspects are well stated and seem to cover the whole arena we have been discussing. Then Campbell adds one more:

- **Myths are essentially for the underdeveloped mind, the youthful mind, in their original versions**.
  When we hit middle age, and the crisis of rethinking our lives that comes with that bodily and emotional change, we realize that the mythic monsters of our childhood are, in fact, externalized versions of the monsters we must now deal with as internal challenges. The boogeyman who was "out there" is now perceived as a fear that truly exists "in here," and needs to be dealt with.[1]

Our childhood myths can certainly help us if we are able to recall them. If we cannot recall them, or anything like them, then the situation hits us with almost unmanageable force and we spin into crisis. In effect, this means that myths are for children, initially, but are most certainly for adults in the long term. As adults we have learned to see them as not "true"; instead, they are symbolic guidance in a language that is suggestive rather than definitive.

If we return to the pubertal rites I described right at the start of this book, the adult males who are involved in dressing themselves up and seizing the young boys, to drag them away from the female compound, know this is pantomime. The mothers who scream and yell and grieve are only pretending to do this, but they know they have to be convincing for the emotional impact to succeed. Only the boys themselves think this is a real crisis. But then they are quickly reassured, and later they can see the usefulness of the ritual. When they, much later in life, hit a time of doubt and confusion (perhaps a midlife crisis of some sort, as their society sees it), they can remember their early ritual. From it they can draw reminders about what it means to be a man, and how to act even in the midst of this new crisis. The old lesson acquires a new depth and value.

This cannot happen if there are no early myths, and above all else it cannot happen unless the early experience of myth is *memorable*. To be memorable, an event must be linked to a strongly felt emotion.

In the bad old days, this was taken to some strange extremes. The tendency to beat pupils in schools was not simply to hurt them but to evoke a strong enough emotion in them that they would remember the moral lesson. The expression still in use today of "beating the bounds" was, in the 17th century and earlier, a physical experience. In it, youngsters were shown the boundaries of the parish that they must not go beyond, and to make sure they remembered it, they'd be beaten on the backside with a birch cane. Not pleasant—but totally memorable! Since going beyond parish boundaries in those days could involve imprisonment in the unfamiliar parish (the usual punishment for vagrants), this was a real lesson that needed to be enforced—although it's hard to have any sympathy at all with the methods involved.

I mention it here because a strong emotion is useful, and ours is a society that has few strong emotions around its myths and rituals anymore. Failing a truly strong emotion, though, pain will serve. I cannot help wondering if this is what lies behind the current enthusiasm for tattoos. One in five people now has one, according to *The Guardian* newspaper in the United Kingdom, and there seems to be no slowing up in their popularity.

Tattoos are about many things, of course. They are often more cosmetic than anything else, and the overriding value of adornment is to assert the identity of the individual and that person's perception of his or her status. The pain of a tattoo (ask anyone who has a complex tattoo on, say the inside of a wrist), the expense, and the emergence of an image or piece of script that is to be seen and admired serve as a form of ritual scarring, which is centered on "an experience" that has been lived through. A tattoo is also, pretty much, permanent. We cannot forget its existence. It's a message we send ourselves about who we are—a daily reminder.

Among those tattoos I have seen, mostly on women, have been texts that repeat words clearly associated with the individual's inner life. The young woman in Maine who had gothic script tattooed along the outside of her leg to her ankle that read "It's who you walk with when you walk through the flames that matters" was expressing a philosophy. The women I saw in San Francisco who had quotations from their favorite authors tattooed on their face or neck or forehead were not ill educated or cheap. They seemed to dress well and possess intelligence. When we look above the eyes of an attractive young woman and read: "What do you see when you look at the windows of the soul?" we are clearly in a realm that is not just small talk.

If people don't have a way to record their important life passages, their sense of their internal changes, or their sense of empowerment, then we tend to find them resorting to forms of self-adornment and even, at times, self-mutilation. This is a very personal expression. It works in exactly the way Joseph Campbell describes, because it is a physical reminder of an inner event and whatever that meant for the individual.

In direct contrast to this, for many people today, strong emotions tend to cluster around such things as sports events, instead. This is a much more public activity than a tattoo. As we know, sports are a powerful metaphor, and a persuasive cultural myth of us-against-them is acted out each time there is a game. This reinforces the tendency to see the world as a place where it's necessary to strike hard and be the best. As we know, though, that's only one way to exist in the world.

The situation, therefore, seems to be that our existing myths and rituals (such as sports) are not always fully connected to a deeper sense of personal significance, but that the content they have to relay is as vital as ever. Time has led us to a place where instead of the myths of our civilization being easily accessible we have to regard them as special communications, coded in styles of dress, adornment, and thinking, requiring specific skills in order to access them. It's a bit like learning Latin in order to appreciate the classics. Years ago, a whole segment of society learned Latin as a matter of course. That's not the case anymore.

The assimilation of myth has now become a somewhat refined activity. Once upon a time, though, it was a normal and everyday action. Every aspect of experience was seen to be a reflection of the myths that dominated that society and culture. Like finding unpasteurized milk these days, it takes a positive effort to find what used to be the norm.

Under these circumstances, we must expect to find some bold experiments and some emotionally charged new ways of approaching ritual. Sculptor Antony Gormley took ritual to a new level in 2006 at Margate, on the south coast of England, when he created an 80-foot-high sculpture called "The Waste Man." This huge figure of a man was created with steel beams, and with the help of the local populace. Gormley, best known for his soaring "Angel of the North" sculpture in Gateshead, asked people to bring waste items or personal things that they wanted to remove from their lives to the sculpture. They were allowed to dispose of only one item each.

The good people of Margate appeared with a huge variety of items—bags of love letters, pages of abandoned novels, unwanted furniture, small sealed boxes of items they had kept for years but couldn't live with any longer. Family heirlooms of surpassing ugliness were handed over to be included in the sculpture. When the steel framework was full, packed with several hundred tons of memorabilia, Gormley invited everyone to attend around dusk, then set fire to the whole thing. The flames leapt into the night, and the spectators cheered and wept, saying good bye to things they had kept in their lives that they knew they had to get rid of, that were weighing them down, but which they had hung on to. The entire moving event was filmed by Channel 4 TV (UK), and broadcast on November 19, 2007 as *The Margate Exodus*.

What Gormley had done was to provide a space, and an opportunity, in which it was acceptable to let go of old things—from ugly sofas to old haunting memories—and do so with dignity. It's anyone's guess how many heartbroken letters and memories he was able to help people to let go of that night in 2006. Perhaps he'll never do it again, and that will be fine. He did everyone a service that night. He reawakened a sense of something larger, something transcendent.

Perhaps we can take something important from all this. Gormley had created a ceremony in which everyone was invited to join. It occurred as a sculpture, as art, but it was clearly also a ritual cleansing. He used art to tap into some of the most primal urgings of people.

Letting go of the past, committing objects to the flames—these are part of a mythic pattern that's been around since human beings first nurtured fires. As far as we know, humans had used fire for several thousand years before we ever thought about cooking with it. Was it a primarily spiritual experience for our ancestors? Certainly, cremations of all kinds figure heavily in our prehistory, and the myth of Prometheus stated that fire was stolen from the gods, who were furious about it. Perhaps fire helped us become human by linking us to the wondrous and the eternal—the god-impregnated dimension of life.

What Gormley did was create an occasion in which the unconscious language, the deep inchoate language of those present, was allowed to break through the conscious overlay of the every day. The "shoulds" of life lead us to hold on to things that the unconscious would rather commit to the anarchic flames of destruction, offering them to eternity and to the gods.

Gormley's sculpture had its predecessors, of course. The wicker men burned by the ancient Celts must have been in his imagination, as well as Guy Fawkes, who is celebrated with bonfires and burning effigies in England each November 5th. It's a tradition that certainly goes back to 1605, and arguably replaces a much earlier pagan ritual held on the same day. Perhaps he also drew his inspiration from Zozobra in Santa Fe, also known as Old Man Gloom. This is a huge marionette who towers above the crowd on the opening night of Fiesta, the weekend after Labor Day. At the end of the evening, he is set alight as a way of dispelling gloom from the past year. This is a relatively recent ritual, created by artist Will Shuster in 1924 and kept going ever since.[2] Then there's Burning Man, of course. These recent rituals, created by artists, tap into and express our psychic needs in a way that defies easy explication.

The Spanish poet Federico Garcia Lorca describes the essence of this sort of ritual when he writes about the *duende*. It's a term derived from the Spanish word for a goblin, that refers to the moment of magic, or peak experience, arising from an artist or performer's skill in creating catharsis in the audience. Lorca uses the word to describe an extraordinary occasion when he witnessed a flamenco singer's incantatory singing driving listeners into a frenzy. This is exactly the effect that Ted Hughes refers to again and again in his poetry and theater work. When we let those demons out they heal us.[3]

Frequently, though, the demons are not quite what we expect.

For instance, a soccer supporter in England made an interesting comment on this whole issue of "winning" in a 2010 National Public Radio news broadcast. He commented that the power of soccer for the fans was not about winning but about the tremendous sense of solidarity felt when your team loses.

> "I think the New World thinks sport should be about having fun,
> you know, about entertainment, whereas football in England and
> in the old football world is about group suffering, pain, and the
> acute sense of identity. Identity is created much more powerfully
> by shared suffering than it is by shared joy, for example."[4]

Then he cited the Liverpool Football Club anthem, "You'll Never Walk Alone." sung by the fans on the terraces for decades. It's a heartbreaker of a song, which states unequivocally that no matter how bad things get, Liverpool Football Club supporters will never abandon each other. It's a song that says, even if we lose we've won, because we won't be divided. It's an extraordinarily powerful anthem, especially when sung by 40,000 Liverpool supporters, standing in the rain, watching a losing game unfold before them.

Isn't that a ritual of solidarity deeper than mere winning? Isn't it something more than success? Perhaps it's closer to the primal cry of "I exist." And if it is, then it's surely stronger than any mere defeat.

This may well be the poetry of the soul, making its way to the surface of our over-regulated lives, as it must do, for repressing it will destroy us. This is why our hearts swell in our chests when we witness the group singing of 40,000 soccer fans who, even when their team is losing, resort to music. This is why the hairs bristle on the backs of our heads at the Palio in Siena, and why stolid citizens weep at the Margate bonfire. This is what Aristotle knew when he saw the audiences of Sophocles' plays swooning.

We know something has happened, something beyond language, and we know it's important. Ritual is the way we contact it.

CHAPTER FIFTEEN

Some Devalued Rituals: Jury Duty, The Drinking Age

I t's 3 a.m. at Anytown College. The campus security phones light up. The dispatch-er takes the call, and a distraught voice at the other end of the line yells for an ambulance.

"Okay. One's on its way. Can you tell me what you think is wrong with your friend?" Her professionally cool response is intended to calm the situation and per-haps get the student to start taking charge of her emotions.

"He's not breathing! He's not breathing!"

"Has he been drinking?" Helen asks.

"Yes, he has. He drank a whole bottle of tequila and then he threw up. Then he drank some vodka…" The dispatcher has already sent an alert to the ambulance and has pressed the code button for alcohol poisoning.

"Most weekends, about this stage in the semester," she says to me later, "we get a couple of these. I wish the drinking age was lower, so these kids could get a little experience with alcohol before they come to college. Take the glamour out of it."

The drinking age in her state is 21. And it is widely ignored by many students who, on reaching college, seem to have one major ambition—to get thoroughly drunk and have something to boast about later.

What we're looking at is not just a college president's nightmare; it's a real situa-tion enacted at thousands of small colleges each year—one that is potentially danger-ous. Every year students die from alcohol poisoning, others start on the first steps of alcoholism, and still others will hurt or kill themselves in alcohol-related accidents, mostly in cars.

Raising the drinking age will not cure this problem, neither will lowering the drinking age. That's because the problem is not about drink or about age; it's about something else. It's about the confused issues of experimentation, rebellion, and independence that are being acted out in this strange way by every generation of youngsters. A new law will not change this or make it easier, yet that is exactly what we'll get. More regulations, more restrictions, and a heavier apparatus of counselors, clinicians, and advisors, all of whom are in the unenviable position of having to deal with the symptoms of something that went wrong long before the students ever reached college.

What is truly at issue here is that, at this age, students in our society are learning, uneasily, how to take the reins of personal power and responsibility. Today, though, this has been mandated by laws rather than by direct engagement with the issues by the students themselves. The rites of passage to do with passing the driving test, taking charge of their lives, and learning how to hold their liquor have been reduced from very personal experiences to a general attitude of finding ways "to get away with it." This is only to be expected from young people at this age. If a law is made, there will always be those who try to wriggle around it simply because it's there. What's missing is the wider dialog about what being responsible actually means.

Long ago the power of alcohol was respected, and sensitivity to its power was an accepted part of the cultural awareness of each society. The Roman god Bacchus, also called Dionysus by the Greeks, exemplified the mind-altering nature of the use of alcohol and was viewed as a powerful god by both Greeks and Romans. Since Dionysus was a god who was seen as the provoker of out-of-control behavior, and even of ecstatic frenzy, the effects of alcohol were not secret or romanticized. The information was woven into stories and thus understood, even by the very young. In every case, though, the myths showed Dionysus and alcohol as being stronger than anything mortals could control. That's a forceful precautionary message.

If we're to understand this situation more fully, we'll have to take a look at another crisis area of our society: the alarming number of traffic deaths involving teen drivers. Various reasons are given—talking or texting on a cell phone, the power of modern vehicles. These are important contributors, but they are beside the point. Today's driving test is something that most young people rush to get through at the age of 16—indeed, they are more concerned with "getting through" than with anything else. For its part, the law says that at 16 years of age, young people are ready to drive, but then adds all sorts of strange conditions. Some states, for example, will not let a new driver drive after nightfall for the first six months, and so on.

Actually, a person may be legally ready and psychologically totally unready for this rite of passage, and no accumulation of laws can make the young person respect the power that is being handed over. Age does not necessarily confer wisdom. We all know this, yet we behave as if we're surprised when young people get into trouble.

I drive to work each day along roughly the same route. Beside the road is a small shrine of flowers and photos hung on a section of chain-link fence. It commemorates the spot where three young men—all college students—died after their car slammed into a concrete wall. Some say the car was traveling in excess of 100 miles per hour. That's a frightening speed on a suburban road. Four hundred yards farther along the same road is a cross, some plastic flowers, and a picture that marks the site where a 20-year-old fellow student died when her boyfriend dozed off at the wheel after going out drinking.

The ancients knew this age was a dangerous one and gave us at least two powerful myths that ask us to ponder this problem. The first is of Daedalus and Icarus. Daedalus, the father, makes wings of wax and feathers for himself and his son to escape from prison. He tells his son not to fly too near the sea or the wings will get wet, and not to soar too close to the sun or its heat will melt the wings. Of course, Icarus is so thrilled by flying that he does not listen. He flies too high, the wax on his wings melts, and he plunges to his death, crashing into the sea. Daedalus can do nothing.

The second myth is of Helios, the sun god, and Phaeton. Phaeton is Helios's favorite son, and the boy knows this and asks him for a favor. Helios, the doting father, agrees, but is horrified when Phaeton wants to drive his chariot, the one that takes the sun across the sky each day. Unfortunately, Helios has agreed to the favor and cannot go back on it; Phaeton insists that he follow through. So the ambitious young man mounts the chariot the next day and whips up the fiery horses. They are too powerful for him, and the chariot careens across the heavens, sometimes too near the earth, provoking drought and forest fires, and sometimes too near the sky, freezing the earth. At last, Jove sees that this cannot continue, for the people on earth are in distress, and he hurls a thunderbolt that kills Phaeton, sending him plummeting into the sea.

Now, it doesn't need much imagination to see that both myths have to do with young men who get power and are too inexperienced to be able to control it well. Icarus simply destroys himself, but Phaeton almost burns up the whole world. In each case, a father looks on while a beloved son is killed through a deed that he, the father, failed to prevent. In each case, the son plunges to his death and leaves behind nothing to place in a tomb, symbolically condemning his spirit to haunt the earth forever.

This is the drama that lies behind the use and abuse of alcohol and vehicles, a drama that every day kills so many of our young people. It's not about more legislation, or better seat belts, or airbags; it's about whether the older generation is handing over power to the next generation in a sensible fashion. If we can't manage to do this with cars and alcohol, then how can we expect the youngsters to do a good job taking over the world of politics and industry? For they surely will take it over, and very soon.

In each myth the consequences of not preparing the son properly, of not allowing the young man to take full responsibility in his own power, are death and destruction. Burial rites were very important to the Greeks: to leave a corpse unburied was both an offence against nature and liable to result in being haunted by the ghost of the dead. These disasters, the tales hint, will haunt us from generation to generation.

The myth tells us what the problem is and urges us to action; legislation, in contrast, leaves us passive. Perhaps we even hide behind the law as a way of not talking about personal responsibility. "Not until you're 16" is easily said but dangerous if the birthday comes around without adequate preparation. We could perhaps deal with this if we had a way of talking to young people candidly about the situation. At one time, that is exactly what these myths were for: to generate discussion of loaded topics in a neutral way. Not only have we lost the myth but also the language that allows us to talk about this stage of life.

Now, it doesn't take too much imagination to extend this discussion to the point where we're also talking about teenagers using guns on each other. It's too easy just to shrug and say it's a problem society has. It's a problem *we* have. We could point out that guns have always been plentiful in our society—violence, too—and that times of great violence and open warfare (think of both world wars) did not, in fact, result in teens gunning each other down in the ways we've seen since the end of the Vietnam War. Peace seems to have bred more violence at home, somehow. Proving a link in any objective, scientific way would be very difficult. Yet when two phenomena arise in close proximity—the explosion of violence in our urban areas and the obvious lack of a mythic or ritual structure among those who seem responsible—then we can be pretty sure there's a link somewhere.

When there's no mythic structure in a society that allows for these topics to be aired, then it tends to lead toward self-destruction. Guns in themselves are just objects, but the machismo that leads youngsters to shoot each other, the drug-related deals that go wrong—all of these are directly related to young men and women who find themselves in positions of power but with no real sense of how to use it.

Let's pursue this topic in calmer waters for a moment. Another aspect of responsibility that is so often shirked is the question of Jury Duty. For many of us this is something that is irksome and inconvenient, and to be avoided if at all possible. Added to this is the fact that if they serve, jurors sometimes even sell their impressions of the trial to the press, especially in high-profile cases, which undermines the integrity of the whole process. Yet those people I have spoken to who have actually served on juries have reported that they felt it to be a privilege to be part of the judicial system. So, why is it that we have so much resistance to doing our civic duty? And why do we feel this way, when the experience itself can prove to be truly worthwhile?

Not long ago, to be selected to serve on a jury meant that one was an upright and valued citizen. Before the idea of a "jury of one's peers" was articulated, only the trustworthy people in the community—those who could think deeply or had substantial wealth—were likely to be asked to serve, in much the same way as an expert witness might be expected to give evidence today. Being a juror was an activity that commanded respect.

Yet, over the years, respect for the law has ebbed and flowed, and today I think that many people feel the legal system is all about protecting large companies from responsibility for their actions, rather than administering fair and even-handed justice. The more cynical among us will say that we get about as much law as we can pay for. Anyone who has visited correctional institutions and heard the inmates speak about this would be inclined to feel the same way. The poor, with fewer resources to hire specialist lawyers, tend to receive longer sentences for the same crimes.

The attitude of many people is that the law is there so that people can sue others for such things as making coffee too hot (the infamous MacDonald's case) and other dubious decisions. So now everyone is looking for what is legal rather than for what is good, moral, or sensible. Corporations are now obliged to put warning labels on consumer goods that tell us not to put electrical items in the shower in order to avoid being sued for negligence if a consumer does something idiotic. This is not a reflection on people so much as it is a reflection on the law.

Originally, laws were introduced as a way of avoiding disputes, not facilitating them. With a law in place it wasn't necessary to hunt down your neighbor if he stole your cow—the law would help you so you didn't have to shoot him. This resulted in more peace and fewer deaths.

Taking all this information together we can move toward some sort of general statement about what it all might mean. When we look at some of the crisis areas in our society—teenagers killing themselves and each other with cars, drink, drugs, and guns, for example—we can choose to see them not as legislative problems or as situations to be regulated but as human growth points that are not being understood.

They *can* be understood, though, if we choose to take a moment and look behind the events to the circumstances that are being articulated through them. In every case, what we'll find is a life passage that is being tackled without adequate support. The myths that could help us with this are missing, ignored, and the rituals have been stripped bare of meaning.

For example, there is nothing emotionally moving about getting your driver's permit. It's neither memorable nor valued by those going through the process. It is hardly ever linked to any deep acknowledgment of the way power is being handed over from one generation to the next. It is rarely pointed out, except perhaps within individual families, that gaining the right to drive a potentially lethal machine like a car is but one step on a journey that will lead to greater responsibility, and eventually to total independence and autonomy for the growing youngster.

Instead of responsibility, what we have is relatively lax laws and ever more stringent and elaborate "safety" issues. Fitting more airbags and seat belts is good, but it's not the answer. Creating the "safest car in its class" is good, but it's dealing with the wrong end of the problem. One of my students proudly announced one day that her parents were buying her a new Volvo. "It's built like a tank!" she declared. And then she went on to say that, at age 20, she'd already wrecked three other cars her parents had given her because she liked to text and talk on her phone when she drove. So their answer was to place her in a safer vehicle, a "tank." The parents paid for everything. How would this encourage accountability and responsibility, I wondered?

CHAPTER SIXTEEN

A Ritual We All
Think We Know:
Graduation

The ritual of graduation is now enshrouded with so many layers of activity that it's almost impossible to work out what actually is going on for the psyche. At the high school level it's linked to the senior prom, to applying for college, SATs, and various local traditions of pranks of various sorts. This has been true since long before director Peter Bogdanovich's *The Last Picture Show* immortalized the last few days of school and graduation on film.[1] At the college level, we have "senior week" and all of the activities legal and illegal associated with the last few days of "freedom." There are presentations, awards, special occasions of recognition, and the list goes on.

All of this can be exhilarating if we are being rewarded, depressing if we are just scraping by and looking at mountains of debt. But we would do well to recognize that this is a transition for everyone taking part, one that involves letting go of what is old in order to make space for what will come. It's therefore a time of some anxiety, and rituals can be helpful.

The heart of graduation is a simple ceremony distinguished by two things: the class orator addresses everyone, and the graduates, dressed in academic robes, get to walk up to a stage, mount it, receive their degrees, and be applauded. For a brief period of time the graduates get to be literally "at the same level" as their professors, applauded by everyone. The class orator reassures them that they are no longer being lectured to but also capable of lecturing back. It is a ritual that is clear and powerful, since it says that the graduates are being welcomed as equals by the adults who have instructed them. Even if the podium is not actually elevated, the student and the president of the college shake hands as the credential is handed over. It's a statement that says: You're ready to take on the world; we've done all we can for you at this point.

96

If we miss this symbolism, we miss so much about the process and the importance of four years of education. It's not about the sheepskin, but about accepting the new graduate as having a certain level of competence (imagined or otherwise). We can focus on the tassels, on the class rings, and the alumni association, the special events and the group photos, or we can see what is going on as a dismantling of a comfortable order of dependence. The significance of the ritual does get lost, though, in all the partying and excitement.

In England, things are even less satisfactory. Many colleges do not have graduation ceremonies at all for those receiving a Bachelor's degree. The entire ritual is omitted completely. My old university, Oxford, a place usually awash in ceremonies of all sorts, will hold an event for Bachelor's degree students, but only if one specifically requests it. There is no individual certificate, and no personal recognition. One lines up with perhaps two hundred others and listens to speeches in Latin. The effect is to leave the new graduates wondering if they had perhaps dreamed the previous three or four years of study. It's unsatisfying for everyone.

I've taught undergraduates for nearly 30 years, and one of the more important things I do for those who are about to graduate is to provide classes in which they can articulate their fears about graduation. Will I be able to manage in the outside world? Will I get a job I like? Will I get a job at all? Has my education given me the tools to cope? What about all my friends? Will we stay in touch? How? Will I be able to maintain my relationship with my boyfriend/girlfriend if he/she moves to New York and I'm in Boston?

These are all surface questions. All of them are important, but all mask the student's basic question: What am I going to do with my life in an open society when I'm used to living in a closed, protected structure? This would be a fine place for a meaningful ritual to "hold" the value for all concerned. Faced with such threats many young students suddenly find themselves getting engaged, launching on wild love affairs, or taking to drink. Faced with freedom, many people will opt for an activity that reduces their freedom drastically, thus solving the problem of what to do next.

Students who have trouble separating from their college experience may feel they have to trash their old college and their old friendships, since that is the only way they feel they can leave. Or they may sentimentalize the whole experience and arrange never, actually, to go out on their own. University towns are full of graduates who just can't quite move on yet. This is especially true of Oxford and Cambridge in England and Harvard and other fine institutions in the United States. In fact, it seems that the better the academic institution, the higher the percentage of people who seem unable to extract themselves after graduation.

It's hard, of course, to leave a place of such social energy, excitement, stimulation, and possibility; yet this has to happen so that the individual can keep growing spiritually. Unfortunately, the amount of debt carried by most graduates ensures that they'll go straight into the best-paying job they can find and stick there as best they can. There's nothing wrong with this, of course, but we could certainly imagine that, for some of these minds at least, possibilities have been derailed by material concerns. We could imagine a different scenario, I'm sure, where young grads go out into the world to do something they feel enthused about doing, rather than something they have to do.

And so this ritual of being launched has a slightly hollow ring to it for many of our finest minds, at exactly the time when they most need more guidance.

CHAPTER SEVENTEEN

A Ritual That Has Endured: Marriage

Marriage is one of the few institutions in our culture that has maintained its ritual function and status. Most people recognize it as an important moment, deserving commemoration in specific ways. Even the instant wedding chapels in Las Vegas have a certain style. They are places where even if you have forgotten the exact and accepted protocols, for a few extra bucks here or there someone will be able to remind you of them and supply you, at very short notice, with everything from flowers to a best man stand-in.

Weddings, of course, are a major industry in our society, with bridal shops and accoutrements, magazines, and, of course, rings. The ancient rituals are still visible through all this, although increasingly hard to see.

One wedding I went to recently had 300 guests for a sit-down dinner of sumptuous generosity, several live bands for the dancing, and matched sets of six bridesmaids and groomsmen. The festivities went on into the wee hours, and the country estate was a scene of memorable festivity. Yet the wedding part itself, from the arrival of the bride beneath the ancient elm trees to the happy pair walking out arm in arm, their new rings in place, lasted a little more than eight minutes. The emphasis was on the party, not the alliance.

If we decode the ritual of weddings, we can find several important hints about what is happening. The tradition of the families sitting on either side of the aisle is not just by chance. It is there to show everyone present that these two people come from two substantial families (this is not about in-breeding, after all), and that such families function as more or less cohesive wholes with their own histories and eccentricities. When one marries one doesn't just marry a person; one marries all that historical and social background, as well. It's easy to avoid this today, at least to some extent, since so many people live so far away from their families. Yet we would do well to notice that who the bride or the groom actually is has been shaped profoundly by this family, whatever it may be. All that DNA and history cannot be ignored. The arrangements of seating are sending a profound message here about origins.

In my own life I have noticed, over the years, just how many of my attitudes and shortcomings stem from my birth family, and my wife notices the same thing about her family, too. We are foolish if we try to overlook these very real influences, even if our helpful, interfering, and lovely (but sometimes infuriating) families would let us.

Similarly, when the bride is walked down the aisle to her waiting groom several things are signaled. The first is that she is arriving in her own time. She has not been forced, coerced, or threatened, or at least that is the implication. She arrives when she's ready. When she walks down the aisle she is on the arm of her father or his representative, who "gives her away." Well, she's not an object that is being disposed of. She is, though, part of a ritual that signifies the transfer of allegiance. From now on, she will be with her husband, and he with her, and their connection will be with each other. Parents must now back away. And they do, by physically stepping back. With luck, they'll remember this later.

As we know, there are plenty of intrusive and unwelcome parental attentions for many couples later in life. There will also be attempts to say unkind things about spouses. "He never was good enough for you," as one woman said to her weeping daughter after a marital spat. This is potentially dangerous territory. Parents are still powerful figures and could, if they chose, ruin a marriage. Yet the symbolism in the ceremony itself is clear: Both partners have left home, now, and their relationship is therefore primarily with each other.

The ceremony also acknowledges another basic fact: Women become pregnant and are no longer able to be such fully effective workers when they are raising children. There simply isn't enough time. The man, therefore, has to play his part—whatever that may turn out to be—so that the children are raised competently. Perhaps he stays at home while the wife resumes her job; perhaps she stays at home, and he goes on with his work; or possibly there is some sort of compromise. But the ceremony has already prepared both people for this. The woman is handed over to the care of the couple, and what the couple needs. This is not sexism; it's simple reality, because it reflects a basic biological fact: during pregnancy, women need care. Later, of course, someone has to deal with whatever children arrive, and that can't be left to chance. It has to be planned for.

And so we begin to see that the ceremony isn't just about a spectacle but reflects some important realities about the new situation that is being entered into by both parties. It also reflects the understandings that are accepted by the whole community to which they belong. The trouble is that unless these symbolic values are alive in our minds they become just so much extra furniture in one's life. That is how ritual dies, and how its value is lost.

The rituals have been lost elsewhere in the marriage arrangements, too. The tradition of the bachelor party or the bachelorette party is now an excuse for almost any sort of rowdy behavior. Lately, the trend in England has been for bachelor and bachelorette parties to go to the Czech Republic. Here, the prospective groom and bride and their friends can separately have an entire weekend of drinking and strippers for very little money, in English terms, due to the favorable rate of currency exchange. This is fine for those who feel they want and need it, although too often the rowdiness is a cover for the sense of panic being felt by the young men and women concerned—a desperate desire to mask fear through bravado.

The bachelor party, however, has a long history. It was popular in the 18th century and earlier as a party given by the groom to those friends he was actually saying farewell to—since he would now have to become a responsible married man. As such it was seen as a "last hurrah," a final fling before the serious business of being a responsible husband descended upon the young man. That is the basis for the drunken and rowdy behavior. Like *carnival*, which was a huge party to mark the last of the winter's preserved meat (*carne*) for some time to come, this was a farewell to the old and hello to the new "diet."

Who, today, really knows that or feels it? Try explaining this sort of history to the people at a wedding and see what response you get.

There is a place for fun and for drinking, of course; yet this should not eclipse the main point, which is that getting married is an act of courage and faith. We do not know exactly what our spouse will be like in the future. Love may last, or it may not. We cannot always be sure about these things, but we have agreed to be with this person anyway. We can't just walk out if we don't like something: marriage is a contract, and it has some pretty strong bonds attached to it. In such cases, courage is absolutely necessary—and the marriage ceremony is all about honoring that courage. What a pity we don't celebrate that more, for without courage there is no love worthy of the name.

Fortunately for us the ritual structure of marriage is firmly in place, and can provide us with the opportunity to reflect on the importance of the occasion because it is, after all, memorable. We call marriage an "institution" because it has so many cultural and social values attached to it, from mother-in-law jokes to the problem of paying for it. Yet it would be more accurate, perhaps, to see it as an occasion when a whole segment of society chooses to buy into the mythology of what it means to exist in the married state, as that specific society conceives of it. At its best it provides understandings and stories that bolster the concept, and that provide ways of ascertaining if the marriage is a good one or not—it links the happy couple to every other marriage that ever was. It generates a series of stories we can tell ourselves about the way the world is, for us. That's exactly what a mythology does.

CHAPTER EIGHTEEN

The Role of the Unconscious
in Ritual Actions –
The Mute Message of Funerals

Imagine watching a grieving relative at a funeral use a trowel to cast a small amount of earth onto the coffin after it has been lowered into the grave. It is a familiar ritual, one we may have seen more often in the movies than in real life, but it can express many things about loss, sadness, and symbolically "burying" the dead person. It can't do that, though, unless we take the time to honor it and revalue it.

As each small handful of earth is tipped onto the coffin it signifies a special "letting go." The grieving person is seen to complete an action that conveys that he or she is agreeing to the burial of the corpse, actively helping to place earth on the casket, and is therefore agreeing to let go of these mortal remains. The relative is saying, publicly, that this person is now being consigned to the grave, that the death has been accepted.

As each mourner repeats the action at the graveside, each is telling him or herself that the deceased is definitely no longer part of this world, and also is conveying to anyone else present that this is the case, thus making it easier for others to let go, as well. That is a significant message. It's also psychologically necessary, since I have sometimes come across otherwise perfectly sane people who talk as if their dead spouse or child were still alive and will come home any minute. Some vital aspect of letting go has not been completed for these suffering individuals.

With this particular ritual gesture the dead relative is, finally, transformed in each person's mind from a living entity into a memory about a person now dead. This is one part of the ritual. The second part is that having the members of the burial party each cast earth on the coffin is also a communication directed toward the dead person, saying, in effect, you have no further role here and we all allow you to depart to the land of the dead, whatever that may be. It may seem to many people completely illogical to send any sort of message to a dead body, yet we must also recall that this is for the living relatives a form of agreement, one they are all endorsing, that they will let this person go from their minds, from their living world of daily concerns. The dead person exists in a different relationship to them now. In our memories, the dead are not dead until we have some form of closure, illogical as it may seem at first glance.

Humans seem to be hardwired to operate this way—in symbolic, ritual actions that express in deed or gesture what can be so hard to put into words. Here, it has taken me several paragraphs of words to attempt to describe one small aspect of a ritual—one that most people understand viscerally right away. The gesture tells us several things. It is important to let go of the dead, or one cannot resume normal life afterward, and so this tiny action, one of many, is psychically important. It also places a vast amount of meaning on a small, economical action. The small, insignificant ritual connects to a larger series of unspoken beliefs that have to do with our complex feelings about death and the hereafter.

Rituals like this operate on several levels. First, they bring the unconscious into play. As a result, in the future, when we find ourselves in a similar situation that has ritualized aspects, we are capable of noticing the ritual elements right away. This then reminds us of other rituals, and we move into a place of heightened sensitivity, where the memories of all previous occasions flood our minds and we become more emotionally alert than we might otherwise be. For example, the first time we go to a funeral we may be feeling numb and confused. The second time it happens we'll notice more, and be able to contact more of the emotions behind the numbness. Eventually, we'll be familiar with the format, and we'll able to use the occasion so that we can, each of us in our own way, feel the feelings and let them go. But we can't let them go until we've felt them.

Sometimes, in slightly different circumstances, this type of response can look like a conditioned reflex, or even mass hysteria. Sports fans, whether weeping or ecstatic, are responding to the occasion but are also stirred by the memories of other, similar occasions. Hollywood does the same thing. We recognize when the tear-jerking moments are coming, and right on cue, we find the tears appearing. This is a learned response to a formula, a type of ritual. Small children do not have it. It's not just because they're young; it's because they haven't had the chance to train their minds to the emotional resonance, so they can't respond.

In a sense, then, a ritual can help us to feel a feeling that we might otherwise not be able to access. After all, an unexpressed feeling may leave us haunted with not knowing what the feeling actually is. In the case of grief, for example, we may not be able to "act on" the grief by feeling it and expressing it in ways that society feels to be appropriate—feeling the sadness of dropping that small amount of earth on a coffin; instead, we may find ourselves "acting out" the grief.

Acting out is almost always unhealthy and misdirected. It's usually about a feeling that, perhaps, we don't know how respond to. So, for example, the confused mourner might show his grief by getting drunk and getting into fights. He's sad but doesn't know it, so he does something that will make it reasonable for him to actually be sad about his behavior. If he has a black eye and a hangover, then sadness and regret will, inevitably, be a large part of his emotional response. He's reached the sadness but may not have reached the real cause of the sadness; thus, it becomes very hard to face it and let it go. He may spend several months getting into fights as a substitute for owning the true feelings. This is exactly what disturbed adolescents do, and what seemingly healthy people also do, with some regularity. They find a substitute way of experiencing what they are not quite sure they feel. The Unconscious won't be denied; the feeling has to emerge, and it's merely a question of how.

Adolescents are worth considering, here, because they are young, feel deeply, and often have not developed the social awareness that allows them to use the ritualized forms of feeling to any effect. It's not their fault. They haven't seen us, the larger society, use these rituals very often, *so they literally don't know how to express what they feel*. This is not healthy. Not knowing how we feel is a major component of not knowing who we are, and if we don't know who we are it's very hard to make reasonable decisions about how to run our lives. From this, we can extract an important truth: Ritual helps us know what we're feeling, so we can know who we are.

Ritual Is Not Always Obvious

Ritual and myth may be a little opaque at times, but that may make them all the more effective. Think of it this way: Real wisdom always has to be felt and experienced, or it won't have value. During a conversation with a wise friend, he or she may tell me some snippet of wisdom I can use. The same thing may happen online. I can look up great quotations by people, from the most famous to the obscure, read them and get a little boost of energy from that. I've also noticed, though, that a few days later I've forgotten many of these quotations; even worse, I'm not using the wisdom in them.

This is because I've not truly *felt* the wisdom; I've merely recorded it intellectually and haven't felt it in my blood, in my heart. This is the problem with such gifts: When they have not been earned by our own efforts, they do not have the same value for us. When we learn a lesson the hard way we *really* know it. Only then can we look back and realize that people had been sharing this particular lesson all along; we just couldn't hear it.

Exactly the same thing happens with ritual and myth. If you've ever been to a ritual celebration that's part of a belief system with which you are unfamiliar, you'll notice that some things seem pretty obvious, and others not so. The function of the ritual and its objects is to contain meanings that need to be thought about and understood. This causes us to earn the meanings, and so to cherish them.

When I first went to India as a very young man I knew that the Hindu temples would have a holy lingam in their center. This is usually a stone slab or pillar representing the penis. Intellectually I knew this, and nodded my head wisely. But when I was actually in India, seeing such phallic posts both in temples and by the roadside, and when I witnessed the reverence with which people offered their flowers and fruit to these stone shapes, or poured clarified butter over them, then I became aware that this wasn't just about sex; it was a solemn and dignified way to think about the creative spirit of the universe. No textbook could have prepared me for that, and as a result my own attitude to creativity, sex, and the power of the universe changed. I think the trip was worth it for that experience alone.

This is exactly how myth works—by being just obscure enough that we have to work at the meanings. Then when the meanings reveal themselves, we feel we truly have earned them.

As a teacher of literature I know this only too well. There is no "answer" to Shakespeare; there is no correct way to read Dickens. All any of us can do is read the stories and ask ourselves how they may apply to our lives. When we see that connection, then the beauty of expression works on us. It imprints itself on our memories. It can't do that without the earned emotional experience. In this the intellect is our great enemy, for the intellect will always try to defend us against truly feeling anything. That is its great gift. We can remain calm (some of us) in the midst of great chaos and sadness, thanks to the intellect. It will help us rationalize, and categorize, and keep us safe from powerful emotions. But the intellect will also stop us from being able to register what the heart has to feel so that we can grow wise.

Let me give you an example of this. At Christmas, a Nativity scene is placed in front of several churches in my neighborhood. They are often large and well-composed groups. The wise men have colorful robes, the lighting is tasteful, the arrangements stylized. But this is a mythic scene that has lost its power, to some extent, for many of us, because we can't feel the situation. It is merely a cliché.

But try walking past one of these when it's cold and raining, with icicles clinging to the facsimile eaves, or water dribbling down onto the plaster figures. Now imagine what it must be like for any woman to give birth under such conditions. Think of what it was like to push the animals out of the way so that the baby could be put in the manger. And why a manger? For one thing, a manger is constructed for hay. It would always be placed in the driest corner of a stable, so that the animals can have dry food, if nothing else. It's a sensible place to put anything that is delicate and needs to be kept dry and warm, like a baby. Now think of how bizarre it would be to have three kings arrive at this scruffy stable, all of it smelling of manure and hay and damp. You can imagine what their servants thought about all this.

Do you begin to get the picture? If we allow our imaginations and our emotions to enter we can get the "meaning"—which is that earth is a truly confused and messy place to be, but God loves us all, anyway. It's not an insignificant message. But we can't get at it if we don't let ourselves ask questions, and feel. Perhaps poet ee cummings put it best when he said:

> since feeling is first
> who pays any attention
> to the syntax of things
> will never wholly kiss you

Words, he suggests, are always a way to try and wrestle emotions into order, and since this is so we must remind ourselves to get back to the feeling—the "kiss," he calls it—because in feeling there is real meaning, which needs to be examined. The intellect will always try to move us toward the cool detachment of words; in contrast, the unconscious will always be based in the feelings. We need the words, but without the feeling there is nothing to talk about.

Myth Can Make Life More Worth Living

This struggle between the everyday world and mythic awareness is not one that can be resolved easily; the two worlds really don't mesh. On a planet where there are disasters of all sorts, it's very hard to think in the terms that myth requires. Yet here's the point: Humanity is not just about survival; it has always been concerned with what makes life worth living beyond the mere fact of survival. The vast population on this planet is evidence that we do survive, abundantly, despite everything that tries to decimate us. So ultimately we are always going to be looking for whatever it is that we consider "makes life worth living."

In my counseling practice, I often deal with people who are looking for love, who feel lonely, and who have resentments against parents, old lovers, and so on. This is not unusual. The popularity of romantic comedies as a film genre seems to indicate that many more people are looking for love and have similar struggles. They imagine that meeting Matt Damon or finding Meg Ryan in their arms will solve all problems, and will take them away from all this.

I'm not sure that's the whole story, though. I think that people look for love because it is a way of articulating the deeper question: What is it that will make life worth living for me? That's a different question. Loneliness, lovelessness, and the sorts of deals we make regarding food, alcohol, compulsive activities, even casual sex, may well be a way of masking this basic question: How do I make my life worth living? The answer, of course, is to choose to see the world mythically. This means that every interaction has the opportunity to be one that is blessed and loving, even when we are meeting our foes. It means that everything we do echoes the larger belief that our existence is worthy and necessary, even if we cannot see the ultimate result.

To do otherwise is to court disaster. The person who cannot see that other human lives matter is pragmatic. After all, with 7 billion of us on the earth none of us really matters that much. Yet I don't see anyone suggesting we suspend the laws against murder, for example, since it is so deeply embedded in us that murder is unacceptable. This is a valued cultural myth, and rightly so. The idea of "doing the right thing" is also a valued myth—although not one necessarily cherished by drug dealers, who value money more highly.

The answer is already right in front of us. Life is already worth living. We just haven't been paying attention to the mythic level of our lives. As Jesus said: "The kingdom of heaven is spread out upon the earth, but people see it not."

If we take that quotation and truly examine it, regardless of our religious background, it is telling us that we're already in paradise (the place that is our "reward" and therefore will make our hard lives "worth living" when we finally die). Paradise is here and now. The Buddha would agree with that, too.

The task then, is to live in both worlds. The first is the practical world; the second is the imaginative world, where everything has resonance. This is a gift we can give ourselves every day.

The relationship between the practical world and the imaginative world is stronger and less direct than we may think. The splendid movie *Invictus* (2010), about events that take place in the early years of Nelson Mandela's presidency, shows this well. As newly elected president of South Africa, Mandela faces a whole series of major political problems. Yet one of the things he does is to make time to nurture the formerly all-white Springboks rugby team, a symbol of white Afrikaaner oppression for many black South Africans.

Why would a politician meddle in such things? For a reason that has to do with myth and imagination. Mandela recognized that a national sports team capable of competing at the international level could help to raise South Africans' sense of their national identity, something that transcended black or white identity. By getting the whole country to rally around the Springboks rugby team, Mandela saw a powerful way of persuading people to accept each other and work together. He also knew that if he disbanded the team or changed it in any radical way, he would alienate the thousands of white South Africans who had always revered rugby, and above all their beloved Springboks. His aim was not to take away a ritual and a myth that a significant portion of the population valued. He decided instead to help make the team something that a whole nation could be proud of, thereby binding blacks and whites together.

Mandela's plan emphasized small but significant things. For example, at the start of each match, the mostly white team was seen lustily singing the new national anthem, "Nkosi Sikelel' iAfrika," the words of which are made up of several lines from each of the five major South African languages; Xhosa, Zulu, Sesotho, Afrikaans, and English. Millions of South Africans watching on television saw their team singing their national anthem with some conviction. The effect was immediate and positive.

No amount of legislation could have created the same impact. Mandela knew firsthand from his years in prison on Robben Island that it is not laws or physical prosperity that solve problems but a sense of spiritual connectedness to whatever it is that makes life worth living for us. Mandela helped a whole country to *feel* that connection. People will starve and struggle for that, so it's never been a question of bread alone. People will die for the concept of equality.

Now, we could say this was just adroit politics, but I don't think that's accurate. People everywhere have always responded more powerfully to a sense of shared purpose than to mere physical comfort. We need this double focus: the small world of the everyday and the world of myth. Without it we can't hope to have meaningful lives.

In this section we've looked at ways to differentiate bogus myths from helpful ones. We've also considered the dangers of casting aside the mythic qualities that could underpin various rituals of responsibility, such as drinking, car ownership, graduation, and marriage, and how we are the poorer, spiritually, for that. Yet each of these events is a rite of passage, and it's easy to have the experience but feel as if the rest of one's time is rather poorly spiritually nourished. So let's look at how myths can work for us on a daily basis.

PART V

The Cost Of Not Embracing The Mythic Aspects Of Life

"Traditions should never be thrown aside without careful examination"
—*ROBERTSON DAVIES*, THE REBEL ANGELS

CHAPTER NINETEEN

What We Can Expect in a World of Weak Myths

At this point we can perhaps begin to make a series of statements about rituals and myths as we have been describing them. A ritual is an action that somehow serves to anchor human behavior, to bring attention to an action as an "event" that has a special importance. These events have survived, in all likelihood, because they have to do with the identity of the group and the individual within that group. They, therefore, have become expressions of some deep, unconscious process that seeks to memorialize itself in some way. It is the preverbal language of the soul that is striving to make its needs felt. No family openly declares, "We eat this way at this table every day because we're showing you the power structure that exists in this family." Instead, we do what we do and the message gets across.

So what does a world look like when there are weak myths and rituals? And why does that even matter?

These are two good questions, and the answers are available by just looking around us. When there is no viable system of myths and understandings about the transcendent quality of the world there is an alarming tendency for things to feel very flat. This is precisely what so many people report—that they have no sense of the wonder of their world, and life seems generally a bit futile. Into the vacuum rush all sorts of substitutes. So, for example, the loss of formal religious belief in Europe in about 1800 led to a compensatory wish to believe in almost anything else.

Easiest to indulge in, in this respect, were stories of vampires, ghosts, ghouls, and nasty things creeping around in the night. The stories of Dracula, Frankenstein, and "the mad woman in the attic" in Emily Bronte's tale *Jane Eyre* all date from this time. Edgar Allan Poe was writing his tales of mystery and ghastliness only a little later, in the 1840s. There is nothing quite like these tales earlier in literature. Today, we still have a massive interest in vampires and werewolves. Enormously successful British import television shows like *Being Human* and the best-selling

Twilight books are evidence of this. As of March 2010, the *Twilight* books had sold over 100 million copies.

So, what's happening? As a rule, horror and supernatural stories of all kinds appeal most strongly to the young. If we think about *Twilight*, the story of vampires who are passionately attracted to each other and to some humans, what we have is a tale that is all about sex and death, and the crossover between the two, where the sexual urge leads toward danger or death. The vampires themselves are glamorous, ageless (of course), feared, and misunderstood. It goes almost without saying that they're always outsiders. In short, they are manifestations of exactly how teenagers tend to feel: alienated, different, dangerous, interested in sex and afraid of it at the same time, and likely to wish to feel alive by contemplating death. That's one reason why so many wear skulls on their clothing, or dress in black, funereal garb, or adopt the goth lifestyle.

The popularity of these books, and others like them, may have to do with the way a teenager's existence in our world is often devoid of any wonder or mystery, because there is no connection to the mysterious cycles of the earth. Into this void, this place of yearning, rushes drama and melodrama. We need what we need, and if society cannot provide it then someone else will.

Similarly, Dan Brown's *The Da Vinci Code*, published in 2003, was so enormously successful in part, I'd suggest, because it took a rather tired mythic structure (Christianity) and injected a whole new level of mystery and complexity into it. Sales figures for 2009 reported that the novel had sold 80 million copies worldwide, and it has also sparked some lively debate about Christianity. The point is that the public seems to be ravenous for some sort of experience of spiritual wonder because they don't get that from the existing religious structures. The Harry Potter series, which has now sold over 400 million copies worldwide, shares many of these traits, and deliberately contrasts the dull emptiness of muggle life with the richness of wizard life. Where life feels empty, spookiness tends to be an antidote—at least for a while.

Emotional Hunger

The resulting public expressions of this desire for drama and mystery can go to some interesting extremes, especially in emotionally hungry young people. On the Web are many examples of such behavior in its more elaborate forms. Take the site called suicidegirls.com, for instance. The name is suitably threatening. The site "celebrates the beauty of women who are not conventionally good looking." In this case, it means they have often extensive tattoos and piercings or even a few mutilation scars, and they appear in melodramatic, provocative poses. *Inked* magazine also celebrates this upsurge of interest in tattooing that, in another era, might have been called excessive.

Now, there are many reasons for people to get tattoos, as we have already discussed, and these are to be respected. Several people I have worked with have chosen tattoos for family reasons—five stars around the belly, or the wrist, for each of the five siblings in the family, for instance. I'm not criticizing these expressions; I'm exploring why this particular expression is so important to them, since it does involve considerable amounts of money and not a little pain. It's hard to generalize, since so many people now have tattoos. We could say that the basic impulse for many people is to try and validate or express some aspect of their life that does not seem to be recognized by others, and this seems to be an effective method.

These inner promptings of the psyche are not just self-indulgent. Quite the reverse. This is the psyche declaring that it knows there's more to life than conformity and preppy lifestyles, but it's not sure quite what. Lacking a viable language of commemoration, of ritual, many people have to create their own. Sometimes that language is frankly masochistic, self-destructive, and depressed. But it is better than not feeling at all, or that is what some people I have worked with claim. In some ways, the complexity of this urge is expressed in Stieg Larsson's best-selling novel of 2009, *The Girl With the Dragon Tattoo*, where Lisbeth Salander's huge ornate tattoo is a statement about who she is and how she has suffered, about what she believes, and why she now rejects most of the rest of the world.

There's more evidence to support this, of course. A particularly interesting form existed among convicts in the former Soviet Union. These "enemies of the people," as they were called, developed elaborate tattoos, created with needles and improvised dyes, that "formed a service record of the criminal's transgressions" according to researchers Damian Murray and Stephen Sorrell. These highly stylized, coded tattoos conveyed information only decipherable by other convicts. In a society that regarded criminals as not being fully human, this was for them an important expression of their right to exist and to have a history. The criminal would show his life story, quite literally, on his body and then move into his place in the prisoners' hierarchy.

Murray and Sorrell record that "the criminal with no tattoos was devoid of status" and was more likely to be victimized. Their research draws on the work of Danzig Baldaev, who spent his life recording these tattoos and their coded meanings. Obviously this is an extreme example, dealing with extremely disaffected individuals, yet in it we see a recognizable basic impulse, one shared by so many young people in the West, today.[1] If a culture doesn't have a viable mythology, it will invent its own, and this is what we are witnessing.

There are plenty of other ways to create a mythology. One is by adopting a very strict version of whatever holy book that culture currently has. This provides a series of laws that give meaning, to some extent, to every life. Unfortunately, for many people, these laws also require the suppression of the self. The extremists of any religion aren't exactly happy with what they have, but they welcome it as being better than having to find their own way. Sometimes, as we know, they find their sense of personal being in anger and destruction.

If we accept that there is a culture of nihilism, of death, and a welcoming of chaos in many different areas of our lives, then it has to come from somewhere. It's not obvious where it starts, yet we can explore some possibilities.

The Roots of Alternate Myth Creation

Why do people today seem to be more attracted to extremism, to self-mutilation and self-hatred? Why do they choose these methods of self-expression? The answers may come, in part, from an unexpected place: our self-hatred is a direct result of the hateful way we treat the earth we live on.

Take a look at the way we interact with our earth and everything on it. We routinely take things from the earth and in the process degrade our planet. When we degrade the planet we degrade ourselves, and we show contempt for our children, and their children, and ourselves. So, for example, we "need" large amounts of oil in our world as it is presently constructed, yet we consume and pollute in a way that does not sustain our planet. We know this to be true. So we are faced with an inescapable problem: We cannot continue this way for much longer. We cannot remain divorced from the earth, snatching what we want at will with no thought of tomorrow, if we wish to survive as a life form.

The unconscious message this behavior sends is that we have no respect for our earth or for other people. We cannot feel this and still have full respect for ourselves.

The young men and women who scar themselves and dress in the way I've described are doing two things at once, in direct response to this. Their actions seem to declare that they have noticed that they don't seem to matter in a callous and brutal society, so it's reasonable to treat their bodies in a way that is, in some ways, a direct echo of the way they feel they have been treated as people.

At the same time their actions make them stand out; they almost compel others to notice them, so they are, effectively, saying that, yes, they do matter, if only to others like themselves who feel the callousness of our world. They can then wear their tattoos with pride, as expressions of a complex situation in which they assert that they are worthy of respect while doing something that, on the face of it, seems to suggest that they expect to experience pain. It's a myth as subtle and compelling as any we've looked at. This behavior is a symptom of what is out of balance in our world, and it's also a rebellion.

The larger society, uncomprehending or unaware of this, continues to destroy and pollute. No one, of course, wants to give up the luxuries of civilization without a fight. Someone else should give up their luxuries first—and so we build the ground for wars or economic exploitations that are every bit as vicious as anything enacted on the earth itself.

But how would it be, though, if we agreed to redefine the nature of success? How would our lives change if we were to reward those who created systems that were not wasteful, rather than rewarding those who create systems that provide excess wealth for a few at the expense of the rest? If we could redefine "what is worth doing" so that it did not rely on amassing money, would we not be in a position to reconsider how we treat the earth?

Think of a modern farmer. He has to produce crops that are plentiful and profitable. The trouble is that, in real terms, food has never been so cheap. In the United States, cheap food is so much part of the expected way of life that undocumented workers are allowed through the borders in order to work at below minimum wage, so that our lettuces and tomatoes can be harvested cheaply. Without these workers the crops would not be gathered, and if treatment of the undocumented workers conformed to American labor standards the cost would be more than consumers would be willing to bear.

So the myth of cheap food and limitless abundance means that farmers are more or less forced to pour extra fertilizers and chemicals on their fields in an attempt to boost yields and stay in business. Sometimes this means that the crops that appear are chosen because they are resistant to the ever-heavier doses of pesticides required, or because they respond well to artificial growth stimulants. These artificial additives raise yield but actually degrade the soil, kill microbiological systems, and eventually prevent the soil from maintaining a healthy balance so that it can reconstitute itself properly. This is a losing game, and everyone knows it.

We could not agree to such a heartless exploitation of natural resources if we were actually aware of what our connection to the soil is. We don't see it, though. We buy products freely from supermarkets without thinking about the real cost of producing them—grapes from Israel, oranges from South Africa, and so on. The carbon footprint, the cost in degraded soil, even the true cost of the oil needed to transport foodstuffs over long distances—all is invisible to us, as well.

I have taught poetry to 20-year-olds for many years. Often, in examining a poem such as Robert Frost's "After Apple Picking," I will ask the class what time of year apples ripen and are ready to pick. On average a class of 25 yields three people who get the answer right. They assume that since apples are always available at the local supermarket, they must always be in season. These are college-aged young people, who will go out into the world to lead it, or at least become a significant factor in making demands on market forces.

When the earth is just something that has always provided, and when other people are simply sentient beings against whom one has to struggle for a job, or whom one has to try hard to impress, then a vital connection has been broken. We have forgotten how we are linked to the bigger cycles of the earth, and what our roles and responsibilities might be. For many people our job is to get the most we can of whatever it is we think we ought to have, at the lowest price. This, in effect, reduces us to thieves, since a thief thinks exactly the same way. If we can get mangoes from Madagascar cheaply, even if it means destabilizing the workforce and causing long-term misery, then that is what we must do, since doing anything else is obviously "crazy." That is a disconnect that we must seek to heal, somehow. To be sure, Fair Trade agreements to pay food producers in foreign countries a decent wage are a step in the right direction, but they are not nearly plentiful enough when compared with the blatant profiteering that still goes on.

These are our most commonly held myths—myths that we don't even truly know we have—and they are out of touch with reality. They are patently absurd, and often dangerous. Consider the following list of questionable assumptions:

-   The earth will keep providing for us forever, no matter how badly we use our resources;
-   Scientists will always come up with a solution, no matter how dire the problem;
-   We'll always be able to drill for more oil;
-   We'll always have new drugs available so we can be cured of diseases, even if they become resistant to our treatments;
-   If all else fails we can colonize new worlds.

This is just a sample of the sorts of beliefs many scientists key into.[2] And they all stem from the basic delusion that the earth will just keep on providing what we need. As a result, we keep helping ourselves and wasting much of what we seize.

We know, though, that we cannot continue to live the way we do. We know that we are decimating the rainforests. The Dust Bowl of the 1930s, when much of Oklahoma, the Panhandle of Texas, and parts of eastern New Mexico and Colorado blew away in dust storms, stripped the topsoil for hundreds of miles and was a man-made disaster. Similarly, until in the mid-1800s, Plains Indians had lived lightly on the land for several thousand years without decimating it. Very rapidly, European settlers killed the enormous herds of migratory buffalo that provided the cornerstone of Plains culture and came close to wiping out the native peoples.

Buffalo herds had supported Plains tribes for countless generations without being noticeably reduced. Tribes killed just enough buffalo to meet their needs each year in order not to threaten the survival of the whole species. Today, buffalo only exist because they have been placed in protected areas, where they roam in relatively small herds—a fragile population, still. The examples could easily be multiplied. The destruction of various species of wild animals, birds, and plants is proceeding at a pace that is frightening, yet we are not frightened enough of the consequences of this loss to prevent it.

We think this way because we are at war with nature. In the minds of many people, the natural world is something to be tamed, exploited, and turned for profit; it is not something we inhabit as we would a house—something that needs to be tended, maintained, and kept in good order. Earth is seen by many people as an object that exists for us to exploit, rather than something that we have to work to conserve in healthy balance. It is seen as "other," when we are, in fact, part of it.

We have to reverse this attitude and change these damaging myths. The answer, then, may be simple, at least to begin with. We could attempt to get people back to the land—get us all working on farms of various sorts. Many countries have used military conscription for a similar purpose, and there is no reason why a year or two of some sort of work of this kind could not be made part of a college loan situation. Some colleges already have farms that students are expected to work on, much as "work-study" is used for more urban students, who presently work only in university offices, often answering phones or filing papers.

The aims of such an outdoors education would be fairly basic. It would be important to show people not just basic things such as where meat comes from but, more importantly, how much food and space a decently treated beef steer needs, and how complex it is to convert meat on the hoof into steaks, patties, and all the other meat products we use.

Raising animals for food will continue to happen, whether we subscribe to the vegetarian lifestyle or not, and offers an important lesson in how much effort goes into raising our food for how much return. Some vegetarians, especially the very young, are "fad" vegetarians, who temporarily feel it is "kinder" to animals not to eat them. This is almost as detached as the mind-set that doesn't care about animals at all, since the locus of interest is all too often not the animals or the system in which they are raised but the way the individual's mood swings in response to a vaguely held notion. It is an attitude that is just as blind to the realities of food production.

If we agree that there is a dislocation between who we are and our awareness of where we came from, then it would be vital to show our young people just how long it takes to raise a field of corn, and what needs to be done to the field first, as well as during the rest of the year.

It would also be important to talk about waste. To a farmer, waste is a real problem, since it has to be dealt with somehow. It cannot be left in a plastic bag for someone else to take away to a landfill somewhere out of sight. People need to be aware of what happens when materials become waste, and I do not think television is an adequate medium to transmit this. Hands-on experiences, complete with all the sounds and smells of food production, would be essential. A farmer has to make space and provision for waste, whether it be an old animal that dies and leaves a carcass or a piece of machinery that has rusted to death.

Is this scheme even possible? Yes, of course, it is. The Israeli kibbutz was a version of this. Not so many years ago young people in almost every community were sent out to help gather the harvests—although this tended to be more popular in times of war. If it could be done in response to national emergencies of that sort, why not in response to ecological emergencies?

My own experience with farming is limited, but perhaps relevant because of that. I'd grown up around farms, worked on them, but not fully internalized the lessons. When I moved to Boston, my city-supplied victory garden allotment was not a success because I didn't put in the amount of effort required. I watched as my neighbors' lots produced astonishing crops, and knew that my half-hearted commitment was not enough. My attempts to grow vegetables at home ran into the unpleasant truth that my urban neighborhood had been a dumping ground for two centuries. Not only was the soil full of building debris and old heating clinkers but it was also poisoned with lead paint and mineral oils that had leached into the space around the houses. I tried growing things in large flowerpots, to no great result. In the end it was easier and cheaper to buy from the store.

Behind this lies a basic truth. When we see how things work and the effort that goes into them, we value them more. When we value them we become grateful, and we begin to appreciate what we have. After my crop planting disasters I look at food differently. Humanity has treated the world, and especially the New World it found on the far side of the Atlantic, as a giant playground in which to behave badly, because all the rides were free. It's time to be grateful. It's time to rediscover the myths of connection.

We've moved a long way in this chapter, from tattoos to farming. The point I'm making is fairly simple. Self-destructive actions, no matter how socially accepted, are alternate rituals that indicate an underlying alternate mythology of despair and detachment. They are heartfelt expressions of an awareness that all is not well. We do not love ourselves because we do not know our earth, and so we cannot love it.

CHAPTER TWENTY

A World Without Coherent Rituals and Myths: Boredom

What is the cost of losing sight of the rituals and myths of our culture? Well, we've already looked at the desecration of the earth, the degradation of the concept of work, and the loss of a sense of wonder. That's plenty to be getting on with. Yet we can look at something far closer to home if we want evidence, and it appears in a surprising fashion. The cost is that we, ourselves, become less than we could be.

One of the topics that bubbles up frequently in my classes and workshops, which tend to be attended mostly by women, is that men, especially white men in the Boston area, are seen as boring, as not interested in looking more deeply into life, and as being ultimately rather limited. A colleague of mine who retired recently, after 35 years of working as a mental health counselor with undergraduates, said that the most prevalent complaint from students he encountered in the years leading up to his retirement was, "They say they don't seem to be able to have fun." They drink to get drunk, or they find drugs so they can appear cool, but they don't know how to have fun just being around each other. They don't even seem to enjoy each other's company that much, on the whole, he reported.

White Male Blandness

Another colleague of mine, who has made a career discussing the dating habits of men and women, has called this "white male blandness." It was a phrase contributed by one of her phone-in listeners on a radio program, and seemed to spark immediate recognition in her other listeners.

This white male blandness comes from what I can only describe as a reluctance in white men (and men of color who aspire to be "white" in terms of the privilege it conveys) to allow themselves to be anything other than successful by the standards of the society they come from. That means the two cars, the "good" white collar job, the house in the suburbs… the whole "American Dream," in fact. To achieve that dream requires focus, and not venturing too far out of the mainstream that wants to reward mainstream people. It requires conformity and hard work.

What does this mean? Perhaps you remember the movie *Titanic*? There, the problem was couched in terms of class and privilege. The poor immigrants in steerage were depicted as having much more life and vitality than the wealthy people in the first-class cabins. The upper classes (on the upper decks) were expected to conform, socialize together, and behave in very restrained ways—and the reward was a dull but opulent lifestyle of marrying according to social expectations. The steerage crowd knew that they had no social position to maintain, but they liked to have fun and be themselves, because "conforming" for them meant becoming invisible, with no actual rewards attached to it. For the lower classes, becoming invisible was simply unthinkable, for they knew that the moment they became invisible to those with power, people like employers, that was the very moment they became open to the worst sorts of exploitation.

In the United States today, we have more and more people who either want to follow the money or who arrive here from desperately poor places to follow the money. Some of these groups will have lively and vital first-generation immigrant lives, but the chances are they will produce children who will be only too eager to buy into the bland status quo. The aim of the second generation is overwhelmingly to "get a good job" rather than create their own businesses or be their own masters. In working for someone else, there is often a tremendous pressure to suppress the self and toe the line.

I see this at colleges, of course, where the most popular major is often Business Management, and where the usual career path following graduation is to join someone else's business, climb the ladder, and make a bundle. At no point does the individual strive to be him- or herself. In doing this, in following the money and not life itself, we can all lose sight of what we are connected to, where we've come from and, ultimately, who we are. Someone who has no idea who he or she is—that's not going to be a fun person.

I have only anecdotal evidence to support my next claim, but I have observed some thoughtful, intelligent women who have found it much more satisfying to form romantic relationships and friendships with men who are not of the dominant "bland" culture, and perhaps who are immigrants. The attraction here is perhaps that people from poorer cultures than ours (which means most cultures) have fewer material objects to distract them, so they have more experience in just being themselves. They have no trouble having fun without needing access to extra consumer durables to help them. They eat, talk, laugh, play cards, and have a wonderful time being themselves. They don't need to go to Vegas to "have a good time." They don't even need to go to a bar or buy an expensive car. All they need are their friends. Most of all, they know how to *be* a friend, which is not an ability to be overlooked.

This is the image we see when we look at films like *Enchanted April*, or any of those movies that celebrate the Mediterranean lifestyle of leisurely eating and enjoying company.[1] It's a robust genre. Think of *A Room With A View*, for example—based on the E. M. Forster novel that was a huge success in 1908.[2] It articulated roughly the same sense of the blandness of conventional life. Forster went on to write other novels with the same theme, which indicates that this was a concern even a hundred years ago.

The 2006 Russell Crowe movie *A Good Year*, based on expatriate writer Peter Mayle's novel of Provençal life, is a more modern example. It centers on a plot in which Crowe, as a successful but lonely financial trader in London, discovers he can find real contentment in France, growing wine, and in the arms of a woman who has no desire to live the jet-set life. The tension in the movie grows around his reluctance to give up his city life and commit himself to the vineyards. Eventually, he decides on a life of rural bliss. It is a lovely, if simplistic movie, yet it also functions as a mythic story. We, the viewers, don't need a vineyard in France to get the message that we might need more real friendship and more of the beauty of nature in our lives. The movie asks us to choose which one feels more vital. One myth can replace another—if we pay attention, and if we take action.[3]

We could criticize the movie and say that it offers us an impossibly glamorous version of reality. The women are always beautiful, the men always handsome, and we don't see hard back-breaking labor going on. This is true. And in some ways that is exactly the nature of a myth: it cuts to the core of the matter, and if realism is the loser then so be it.

As we recall, those early myths with centaurs and dragons are hardly "true" in any literal sense, nor were they expected to be. Instead, they describe a spiritual problem and its solution. In this movie, the character played by Russell Crowe takes a long time to see where he truly belongs. He's a reflection of many of us. We know what we need, yet we don't always take the steps we ought to, at least not right away. But the possibility of doing so is always there.

PART VI

Everyday Myth: Finding Soul Sustenance To Get You Through Each Day

How else but in custom and ceremony
Are innocence and beauty born?

— *W.B. YEATS*, A PRAYER FOR MY DAUGHTER

CHAPTER TWENTY-ONE

Work: Burden or Ritual Opportunity?

One of the most time-consuming activities for everyone is work. We spend large portions of our lives at work, preparing for work, and commuting. Work is, therefore, a major preoccupation at every possible level. Even so, many people can't drag themselves out of bed each morning, loathe their commute, and complain bitterly about their jobs. "It's just a paycheck." "It's what I do until I retire." These are phrases I'm sure we've all heard.

Work, though, could be more than just a way of filling the day. The problem is that most of us feel divorced from anything meaningful about the work we do. Many of us are aware that we work for companies that seek to persuade people to buy products they don't really want, don't actually need, and at a price that's well above the actual worth of what is delivered.

This is true to some extent of even the finest products. I don't really need the latest version of whichever cell phone is fashionable, but everyone seems to say how useful it is to do certain things (even if I'd never even thought of doing them, and probably never will). I know, though, that I don't really need this new cell phone, and if I don't buy one, my life will not be much the poorer on the whole.

To take an example closer to my own experience: I work in a college, and much of what I have to say is true for all colleges like mine. Many of my fellow professors are idealists of the highest order. They believe in what they do and in the necessity of educating people to help create a better world. They talk ardently and at great length about what the true purpose of Liberal Arts might be, and how to get students to think in new ways.

The administration, on the other hand, seeks to make money for the college. That is its job. And if that means skimping on those courses my colleagues in Philosophy and Fine Art regard as essential, then so be it. In the name of attracting new students during changing times, experienced teachers may be "retired" and a new emphasis placed on teaching "marketable skills" that will get the graduate a job.

It's not hard to see that these two groups, administrators and professors, barely speak the same language. Of course the college has to make some money or it won't continue, but it also has a mission to deliver quality. The professors (if I may generalize) tend to be those who believe in their work and often work for low pay because at the end of the day they feel they have done something good. Administrators get rewarded for saving money. It's not hard to see the contrast in world views.

It's a good example of the clash between the old way of doing things, where a person found meaning in work, and the newer way of doing things, where we find reward in the salary and what it can buy. The first way of doing things is sadly fragile. We might use farmer-poet Wendell Berry's distinction and say that the educators are acting as the "husbandmen" of the next generation, bringing them to responsible fruition, whereas the administrators are the exploiters of the situation—providing paper credentials at a competitive price. The professors themselves see this split and realize that, ultimately, there's a real danger that students will be short-changed (in their terms) around the business of human values and how to live them.

Husbandry and the Use of Resources

Let's stay with Wendell Berry's distinction for a moment. Like the "husbandmen" of education, the farmers of previous ages did not seek to see how much they could squeeze out of the land. They took care to make sure they didn't take too much so that the land could continue to sustain both itself and them, year after year. This is good. But modern definitions of farming might require two bushels of fertilizers and chemicals to produce one bushel of grain, in the process degrading fields, waterways, and micro-organisms beyond repair. The yields are excellent but not sustainable.

For now the chemicals are cheap, since many are made from the byproducts of oil. Unfortunately, as we all know, oil is becoming expensive—not just in terms of per-barrel prices but in terms of the expensive military actions that have to be sustained in order to keep the price low. We'll have to pay for it all, at some point, so the low price is being artificially subsidized in ways we may not at first recognize.

This sort of short-sightedness was not always the case. In the dark ages, otherwise viewed as a very backward time, each field worker gave his labor, and in return was allowed a strip of a field to cultivate for himself. He was responsible for his part of feeding the whole community, and also for supplementing his family's food.

This led to a way of thinking that was careful and circumspect about land use. Some of their thinking is astonishing to us today. Noticing that the forests of oak trees were being felled to build ships and houses, King William I of England, who died in 1087, decreed a planting campaign to make sure that in another 200 years there would be enough hardwood trees to replace what had been destroyed. That forest, planted nearly a thousand years ago, is still known as "The New Forest," and it continues to flourish in England today. Its oaks are now in their third generation at least. Can we today claim to be thinking 200 years ahead in anything we do? I doubt it. And this seems especially true in education, where the emphasis is on responding to the ever-changing demands of the job market, because people need jobs and need them now.

The notion of husbandry does still exist, even as many of our farms are turned into factory processes and agribusinesses. It is reflected today in the tendency of urban communities to have allotments or victory gardens, in which citizens grow their own food. In Victorian times, workers might well spend all day in a factory or down a mine, but many also had small gardens and often a pig fattening up. People were linked to the soil directly, since it represented food and survival. In turn, this created a respect for the nature of the individual's relationship to the earth, and to the community.

Unfortunately, most urban dwellers today feel no sense of belonging to the soil, or a connection to what it takes to create food for oneself. They cannot imagine being able to create a life that doesn't include having a job where they work for someone else. Yet for generations people lived by gathering wild foods, growing their own foods, and held a job (doing work at home—the original meaning of "cottage industry") only to raise some extra money. As a result, losing a job was not the personal financial disaster it now is, although it could cause hardship. These people were connected with the soil and the seasons in a way we find hard to imagine today.

Work for many people today is something that either helps us "get ahead" or "survive"—but it does not in any way connect us to anything beyond that. Removed from the soil, we have been removed from a strong tie to a mythic sense of living, to which we used to have direct access. Our lives may be easier and cleaner and more convenient, but they run the risk of being far shallower.

The monasteries of Europe had signs painted or sometimes made in wrought iron, which read, LABORARE EST ORARE ("To Work Is To Pray"). These signs appeared above the doors of the kitchen gardens or on the gates that led to the fields. Inside the church or chapel porch was often another sign, its mirror: ORARE EST LABORARE ("To Pray Is To Work"). If work was felt to be a holy thing, then everything one did was a way of linking to the divine. Working at even the humblest task became a meditation upon the nature of a connected world, in which every action had its place, and in which shoveling manure was just as valuable as selling produce for a good profit. And even praying was not an excuse to relax: It took effort to stay focused.

The nature of work has been sadly altered in our modern world. Many people cannot describe what they do in terms anyone outside their immediate industry can understand. I have colleagues working in the technical side of publishing and broadcast media and they report that their families simply cannot understand what they do. Inevitably, these workers have no vital contact with the earth that supplies their needs; now they are estranged from their families, too, as the barriers of understanding seem too difficult to remove.

CHAPTER TWENTY-TWO

What Sorts of Myths
Do We Need?

The question that arises now is: How do we achieve meaningful lives that are centered in a sense of myth and connectedness, not just to the past but to what is deeply important about the past? It's easy to get it wrong. Nations everywhere have identified with a past that is simply dangerous. After World War I, Germany saw itself as "wronged" and so threw itself into World War II, using 19th-century composer Richard Wagner's adaptation of the ancient myths in The Ring Cycle as a model for its plans, with an added twist by Dr. Goebbels. It all worked disastrously well. If nothing else this tells us how hungry we can be for myths, however weird.

The Croats and Serbs felt the same things and set about trying to destroy each other in the Balkans in the 1980s and 1990s, backed by nationalist stories of prodigious vagueness. Meanwhile, today various fundamentalist sects across the globe see themselves as possessing the only "truth" and conclude that everyone else must be destroyed. This powerful feeling comes from the longing for a deep mythic truth—one that has unfortunately been perverted to serve less noble ends.

Propelled by myths, humanity has often taken leaps forward and then tumbled back into benighted existence. The Crusades were certainly a reflection of a longing to be part of a mythic battle to spread Christianity to the Holy Land. The assault pushed Arab learning about science, mathematics, and astronomy into the background, from which it took hundreds of years to recover.

The Fall of the Roman Empire and the Dark Ages of Christian and pagan warfare did a similar disservice to Roman and Greek learning. In fact, we have no guarantee that our world of learning and enlightened discussion will endure either. Yet it certainly cannot endure at all if we don't have a well-developed belief system that goes farther than sectarian squabbles. We need myth more than ever before—not to tell us lies but to show itself openly as myth, as a way of apprehending the eternal struggles in the human heart in a way that can be talked about, discussed, and explored without fear of anyone being branded as a heretic.

What sort of myths do we need? Joseph Campbell suggested that we will have new myths, created by the poets of our time. It's a charming notion, yet not one that I feel is accurate. Myths do not have to be objectively true or even true to life to convey what they need to convey. An example of this is that the Catholic Church has only recently apologized for quashing Galileo's ideas about a universe in which the earth goes around the sun, rather than the other way around. Of course, no one in recent times in the Vatican actually believed that the sun moved around the earth, in violation of observed and demonstrable science. I doubt that any of them believe the earth was created in seven days, either, but no one has officially declared this. Hindus do not really think that the earth is supported on the back of a giant tortoise, either. We could multiply examples of myths that we know are outdated, but which still talk to us at a profound level *because they are myths.*

Can we imagine, then, a world in which we wake up each morning, look at the sun, and remember that not only is it a ball of flames 93 million miles away but also a symbol? As such, it reflects a fact—plants need sunlight—and also a spiritual truth: We receive energy from a miraculous power, and it helps us to grow spiritually. The plants that it creates help us to grow physically, too, so that we can be spiritual beings. It doesn't take a lot of imagination to start thinking this way. But it does require *some* imagination. Alas, our world does not nurture this form of imagination, and we are the poorer for it.

When dawn came, the ancient Egyptians, for instance, didn't just celebrate the sun god Ra, a force of nature that made their food grow. They saw Ra, and also every previous pharaoh who had, upon dying, become one with the sun god. The spiritual world, the natural world, and the political world were thus inseparable, and every worshipper felt connected to a wider sense of the order of the universe as they understood it. The myth reassured them that the heavens had a coherent pattern; that the earth's productivity was part of a divinely regulated system; and that political and social life on earth was inextricably part of this, too. That's an impressive mythic structure.

By contrast, we take the wonder out of our worldly existence in many ways. We do it when we turn farm animals into units to be processed at the most advantageous rates, thereby condemning chickens, sheep, and cattle to specialized farming methods that have no respect for life and total reverence for money.

This is not news. The question that arises, though, is whether our remoteness from something as fundamental as our food has also led us to a remoteness from the wonder of life?

This is not the same thing as sentimentality. The wonder that any farmer experiences is mixed with the cruelties of nature, harshly felt. The crop destroyed, the herd stricken by disease, the need to butcher one's own food—these are not easy or gentle lessons. They were at the heart of our ancestors' lives, though, and are very distant from ours. The cow that was slaughtered was a creature the farmer would have known perhaps all its life, as a large, gentle, sometimes bad-tempered equal. Now, I'm not suggesting we get on first name terms with our local dairy herd. I'm suggesting instead that we would not treat our earth as poorly as we presently do if we were in a different relationship to it.

Honoring The Mythic

What, then, would your daily life look like if you were to honor myth and ritual? Well, on waking, you could start by imagining the sun as a vital part of your life. You could also recall the legends of Icarus and Phaeton and their struggles with the sun, in order to remind yourself of the temptations and possible consequences of taking on power you can't handle. That might be a good way to start the day.

You could continue by eating food that is recognizable as food, rather than as something processed. Try eating things that do not come from a packet, or better yet try not buying some sort of commercially created drink, which has been disguised in a million ways. If you rush into your local store and snag the latest fashionable flavor of soda or coffee, are you any closer to appreciating what you consume?

You could make your own lunch, carry it with you, and eat that instead of energy bars or cafeteria foods. Be aware of what you eat as a natural substance, not just as something you shovel in and forget. Wrap your lunch in something biodegradable or reusable, and then recycle it. Be aware of waste, especially shiny commercial wrappings and water bottles, both of which are practically immortal and will remain as pollution long after we're all dead.

I think you can see what I'm proposing. When we become mindful of what we're doing, it's hard not to feel gratitude for the abundant place we inhabit. It's also hard not to notice the callous way we have exploited so much of the plenty of this earth. That feeling, too, is a type of reverence; which in its turn moves us towards love.

Reverence is always a possible response, even in the most everyday ways. For example, when we take a glass of wine the ritual of clinking glasses and raising them to each other is, in fact, a version of the ritual in which the first sip of the drink is traditionally offered to the gods above. And then all those present drink—but only after each person in the group has been acknowledged either by the clink of rim against rim or by making eye contact, or both. It's a moment of mindfulness, of gratitude, and of community.

We exist simultaneously in the mundane world and in the mythic, transcendent world. All we have to do is slow down and recognize this. In Greece, you will sometimes see people sprinkle or pour a little wine on the ground before drinking—an offering to the power of the earth that brought the vines to harvest. In polite society it is sometimes sufficient to knock the bottom of the glass against the table top, in deference to the gods of the earth. It's hard to forget where we come from if we do these rituals.

In the Mediterranean, fishermen will frequently paint a picture of an open eye on the front of their boats to ward off the evil eye. This is a custom that is rather hard to unravel precisely. It's definitely pre-Christian. The general sense is that the eye will ward off any evil thoughts that may come from those who are jealous of the fisherman's luck. But beyond that there is a sense of wanting to placate the spirit of the ocean that provides the fish, for it may become jealous, also. At its most fundamental the symbol acknowledges that nature is powerful, and the ocean needs to be respected whenever one ventures out onto it. The eye suggests both reverence for those powers, yet also that the boatmen have a right to intrude into the ocean.

In a similar ritual, coastal communities in Sardinia and Italy still sometimes take the sacred Christian statues out of their churches once a year and wash them in the sea. It's a ritual cleansing that matches the Christian religion with a respect for the old gods, such as Poseidon. This sort of ancient, somewhat fossilized ritual is still available today in rural communities. It is less readily seen in the United States, where the early white colonists from Europe, some of whom had already set aside their own folkways in their native countries, set about repressing the folkways of American Indians without bothering to understand them first.[1] The Puritans in New England were particularly dismissive of the American Indian ways and beliefs, which they saw as unchristian and wicked. Their energetic repression of what they found is one reason so little remains there today of the earlier culture.

In fact, the Old World may have plenty to teach us. In Europe, for example, wells were almost always sacred, as were rivers. Churches were built on the sites of pre-Christian temples so that the ritual washing that had been part of that earlier tradition would be honored by having the church near a water source. The Great East Windows of churches were aligned with the direction in which the Holy Land was perceived to be, but also so that the offerings could be made in the light of the morning sun—as was the druid and pre-druid custom. When we know these layers of resonance, it becomes impossible not to be alert to the mystic and the mythic dimensions of life, because they are woven into what we do and who we are.

Walk through any English town and you'll come across street names that remind us of sacred water sources, even if the wells themselves have long been built over—Holywell Street is a fairly common name in England, commemorating a water source that had been revered perhaps for centuries. The river Thames itself is in fact a contraction of *Thame Isis* ("The River That Starts at Thame That Is Sacred To Isis"), which was the closest the Romans could come to an understanding of the local goddess. Fleet Street was named after the river that was long ago channeled through underground pipes. The life-giving water source was revered, even as it was removed from public use. And there are many more examples. When our local landscape becomes, in this way, part of a mythic belief system it is hard not to live according to its promptings.

This sort of awareness acts upon us in the same way as a palimpsest. We are simultaneously aware of many layers of resonance and meaning, while being in our busy present. Yet we can only be aware of those meanings if someone has taken the time and trouble to alert us to them. Otherwise how would we know?

The Australian Aborigines have an extremely strong and ancient custom, in which walking routes across the country are marked by certain geographical features associated with various stories known by the tribe. The practice is described in many places, particularly in travel writer Bruce Chatwin's book *The Songlines*.[2] Aboriginals will literally sing their way through the stories and legends of their culture as they work out which route to take. The whole landscape has, for them, a mythic quality that has nothing to do with global positioning systems or compass coordinates. The landscape is alive.

At the far end of the world from Australia, in Iceland, there are local myths and legends that are similarly strong. Planners and road construction teams often have to redirect the planned roads in order to avoid spoiling features in the landscape, in some cases because the features are thought to be sacred, or because elves are believed to live there. I can't imagine that happening in the United States, for example, with its big companies pushing highways through wherever they wish.[3] The point is not whether one believes in elves; the point is that there is a reverence for the mysterious nature of the landscape, the beauty or power or strangeness that is expressed in the idea of elves. For which of us has not felt the power of certain landscapes? Which of us hasn't felt that there is a spirit in the land?

A more usual attitude is that which is reflected in Europe. A road is pushed through farmland, and if any archaeological remains are found, then the local authorities are alerted and road-building stops temporarily. Sometimes a project can be held up for a month as the archaeologists work feverishly to survey everything before the tractors come in again. Clearly, this is not a perfect system. Greedy contractors don't wish to report any finds they may uncover, and so they tend not to. And in the end the sites are reburied very quickly. So, the landscape is honored, in one way, while the destruction continues. Along the way the power of the landscape to move our emotions, to connect us to more than just ourselves and our need to travel between cities fast, has been eroded and lost. Fortunately, we do manage to preserve some of the past, and the benefits are readily felt.

The effect of revering the landscape is to keep us constantly reminded of the divine, and the divine nature we share, even as we live in the mundane world of doing what we have to do. Everywhere there are links to the eternal, if we pay attention. The "experience" of Europe, for example, is not just of different languages and unusual foods and drinks. It's not just that they have different cars or traffic regulations. It's that, at one level, they are capable of being in daily direct contact with a sense of history, a depth of meaning, that we in America may not be familiar with. It doesn't mean that there are no ignorant, greedy, or stupid people, of course. It just means that the mythic is closer to the surface of life there. And as we become more caught in our material comforts in every corner of the world it becomes harder for us to see that which is not material.

Perhaps the best way to find the myths we need is to be thoroughly awake to the landscape we move through. It will inevitably cause us to love the earth we walk upon, and, in the process, to love each other.

CHAPTER TWENTY-THREE

Rituals of Food:
Dietary Norms
and Strictures

With our new sense of alertness to the possible mythic values of what we see before us every day, let's take another look at the ways we treat food. Attitudes to food are often surprisingly different throughout cultures, and they reflect a sense of a group or an entire people telling themselves, and others, who they are. We are people who eat this, but not that.

So British people, when they wanted to insult the French, used to refer to them as eating snails and frogs, which was a way of saying that whoever Britons may be, they certainly don't do that. Britons are also rude about their own regional eating habits. Tripe and onions are "northern" dishes that no southerner would touch—and so on. This is simply prejudice.

Diet also works as a sign of being different in another way. Jewish dietary laws, including the strict laws about what can be stored where, are all about reminding the person observing them that he or she is Jewish, with all that goes along with it. It is a social reminder, but also a spiritual reminder. The customs are to be followed because of things that were laid down in the Torah, in holy script, that correspond to teachings and stories. For Muslims, Ramadan has the same value, although the laws are different, and the customs are specific, with regional variations in some cases. For Christians the same sort of laws are in place, even though "fasting" at Lent is largely a thing of the past. Many people do engage in a symbolic fast of some kind—perhaps they give up chocolate or some delicacy for the entire period. In each case it is a statement about group identity, and about spiritual foundation.

And yet, how often we forget this dimension. Today, for many people, "dietary strictures" simply refer to what they feel they must refrain from eating in order to stay thin and look good, or to lower their cholesterol.

Family Dinners

Family dinners, where everyone sits around the table and eats and talks about the day, are comparatively rare now, but when handled with care they can be far more than just a bore in which the kids are forced to eat their broccoli.

So let's imagine a stereotypical family dinner. Everyone has his or her designated seat. Dad sits at one end of the table and Mom at the other, usually nearest the stove. Kids are arranged where they either help each other or at least won't squabble. It's like something out of a 1950s TV show.

What's important here is not the cliché but the structures of family living it presents. The arrangement says, in effect, that everyone has a place at the table, a role in the order that is family. Dad, who has been working elsewhere all day, gets to assert his position and to compel a certain amount of respect. Mom, who has probably been at home for at least part of the day preparing the food, gets to cede her place to his authority, while demonstrating her ability to provide food. Everyone has to cooperate, and all have to be in place at the correct time, usually with hands and faces washed, too. What was simply a convenient way of doing things—getting everyone fed at about the same time—becomes a ritual in which they all are confirmed in their sense of where they stand in the pecking order. Perhaps even more important is that the parental efforts are respected, and the hard work associated with cooking and food preparation is fully visible. The kids may not like the green beans, but they can't deny that real effort has been put into producing the meal as a whole.

Now this sort of meal acts as a reminder of so many things that it's easy to forget just how powerful the messages are. If Dad goes to the office, the rest of the family never gets to see him at work, or know whether he works hard or not. If Mom always buys takeout, as happens in some families, then no one has a sense of what the food costs in terms of labor to get the money to buy it, or in terms of the effort to prepare it. No one gets the satisfaction of producing a good meal or getting to show appreciation for the food. It just arrives.

There are plenty of things wrong with family dinners in some families, of course. Ask any group of people to jot down their memories of dinners, and you are sure to find many horror stories. My own family dinner memories are not the happiest overall, so I'm not idealizing anything here. But the act of gathering to eat can function as an opportunity simply to be with others, even if nothing very important is discussed. It's a chance to check in, be seen, and join in. It's a rallying point in the day. At its most primitive it's simply a chance to check that everyone has, in fact, come home, alive and in reasonable shape, before settling down for the night. It holds the shape of the family.

With these expectations around where we stand in the life of the family there comes a sense of "this is how we do it." Thinking like this asserts a sense of identity for the family and each member of it, in which particular values are upheld, no matter how petty. Values can even be rejected or challenged, and they will probably be contended over the dishes of the family dinner. The dining table becomes a form of temple space in this respect.

In short, such occasions, daily repeated, have all the same qualities as any religious ritual. Some even include a short grace, and so they are a prayer ritual, in fact. If we're not prepared to acknowledge and cherish this sort of ritual we may find that a focal point of the family's sense of identity is removed. It may be more convenient to have everyone eat at different times; it may even be less confrontational, and so we may be happy to avoid those shared meals and tense emotions. Yet we can also say that even in a confrontational family there are likely to be some important struggles that are trying to work themselves out, and not having a place to center them is, ultimately, a loss. Growth and perhaps understanding can come from arguments, and some arguments are necessary. Avoidance, by contrast, can grow nothing useful. Rituals do not have to be reassuring, comfortable, or even pleasant in order to be useful. Sometimes it is the very ordinariness of the daily ritual that causes us to discount its real value.

CHAPTER TWENTY-FOUR

Underappreciated Rituals – Cars, and Kitchens: Establishing Our Ritual Space

In the previous chapters we looked at how we've become estranged from any sense of the earth as something we need to respect, and how damaging that can be. Looking after our own personal environment seems to have suffered a similar fate.

Housework is not really most people's favorite activity, which always surprises me because keeping our living environments clean and in good order is such a basic way of showing respect for ourselves that it seems as if it ought to be something people enjoy as much as, say, taking bubble baths. Taking a bath helps to keep the body in good order, so it's not a silly comparison.

Housework, unfortunately, has suffered some vicious attacks over the years. The proliferation of "labor-saving devices" and machines designed to take the "drudgery" out of housework are very welcome; yet, by viewing housework as drudgery we are declaring that no one would do this type of work if they could get a machine to do it. We might also believe that if there is a machine to do the job once done by the "housewife," it suggests that she is, herself, not doing a particularly useful job—after all, *it can be done by a machine.* So it can't be truly valuable, can it?

If we step back about 100 years, it would be fair to say that for many households the very survival of the family or economic unit depended, almost directly, upon the housewife being extremely skilled and ingenious in a large number of particularly diverse occupations. The woman—for it usually *was* a woman—had to know how to do hundreds of operations, from buying food on a budget and canning produce, to sewing and making clothes, to knowing how to keep a home clean so that vermin did not invade, and how to raise and doctor children and adults.

If a housewife was not proficient in these skills, the chances of dire poverty overtaking the household were much greater. The men of the house were also expected to be competent in repairs, in doing the heavier work, perhaps in planting and raising a successful vegetable garden (not easy, as I've already pointed out), and various other tasks, including supplying the home with fuel.

Housework was hard work, but it was useful work that required intelligence, skill, planning, and a considerable amount of knowledge. It was not "drudgery" in the sense that the advertising world wishes us to consider it, and it did, in fact, command respect. Work was valued, and in the valuing it became a real gift that each person brought to the home, a contribution. Doing the chores was not a bore; it was an expression of belonging to a home, and a sense of responsibility, even pride, for being in that home. Everything the householder did, under such circumstances, had the capacity to be a ritual, a claiming of ritual space.

Of course, even during those generally house-proud days, disorderly homes did exist, along with squalor, filth, and desperate circumstances. But if we look at those unhappy scenarios, we discover that they tend to be urban experiences, usually linked to a family's inability to do things for themselves because of the immediate environment. Slums and ghettos often had no kitchen gardens or other means of aiding in personal survival. As a result, slum dwellers could not survive without a job (work done for others for money), and a job loss meant almost immediate poverty for many people.

The need to earn money to buy things took the place of skills for survival. Millions of workers in the newly industrialized world, men *and* women, found that they only had one skill—their physical labor—and they had to sell it to a factory that only wanted a very small amount of their ability. The assembly line didn't use a human being's skills; it used just one skill, perhaps merely the ability to paste on labels.

The degradation of the idea of work from something that is interesting, demanding, useful, and necessary to the repetition of rote actions started right there. At the same time, the idea of "home" was also degraded, reducing the space people lived in to its most basic. It was a place one rested until the factory whistle blew again.

Industrial countries were the hardest hit. In countries where much of the population was engaged in rural and agricultural work (such as France), the ability to survive without just being a wage slave remained in effect. In the industrial cities of England, workers ate the cheap, processed foods that were all they could get hold of, and their interest in eating well was reduced to the idea of "meat and two vegetables."

But French cuisine never lost its connection to its inventive rural background, and to this day the food is better as a result. When wars hit and food was rationed, the inhabitants of the French and English countryside were able to be inventive and resourceful with what they had, whereas city dwellers were not so fortunate. The unpopulated sections of the countryside are still full of mushrooms, fruits, and plants that can be picked for free, if you know what you're doing. The wild food movement in England is about exactly that, and has many enthusiastic adherents. They go out on weekends and gather seasonal berries and plants that normally would be ignored or considered weeds, and make tasty, nutritious, organic meals that can help to feed the family all week. One cannot do this in the city.

Unfortunately, this freedom to gather local fruits is no longer the case in much of the United States, too. As a friend of mine who lives in the countryside says: "This is the country. All the good food gets sent to the cities. My corner store has canned vegetables only." And he's right. In many rural towns, the small village store sits alongside acres of cornfields and has a pitiful selection of fresh food, mostly imported apples and oranges. Either you grow your own fresh vegetables or you do without. There is no public land or wild land that isn't turned over to the cornfields. There aren't even any hedgerows. This is a far cry from the bustling villages of France and Italy and Germany, exploding with fresh produce, regional specialties, and odd items that the locals consume with enthusiasm.

The degradation of food, like the degradation of work, hinges upon the domination of cash. We sell our labor for money, then have to pay someone else to do what we might otherwise have done for ourselves because we're too tired or too unskilled. The unskilled laborer drawing minimum wage has to buy the cheapest food available close to home, and probably has no time or allotted space to grow any food. Inevitably, the quality of cheap food suffers, since it's being produced in order to create maximum profits at the lowest selling price for people who have no other option.

There's no reason why we can't reverse our approach to food in our own homes. But it takes a lot of effort to do so because "advances" in processing have automated food production and made life so much easier. Why grow your own vegetables when you can buy a tin cheaply? Why make a cake from scratch, when you can buy a mix, put it in a machine, or simply buy the finished cake ready made? In the name of "convenience," we've moved from being able to do things for ourselves and become, instead, "consumers" of manufactured "products."

But we can reverse that. We can turn getting our food into a personally rewarding activity, if we wish. We can select our own fresh food, or grow it, and invite other family members to be part of that process of cooking and preparing. We can do it. But we don't have "time." Wrong. We have the time (we spend it in front of the TV, mostly). We just don't see the ritual and redeeming aspects of this "work." This kind of work is a dirty word to so many people. It doesn't have to be that way.

We can always choose to see household tasks as a confirmation of the value we place on our home environments, if we shift our gaze from the acquisition of things like wide-screen TVs and think in terms of making our own space an expression of personal values, filled with objects we have helped to create rather than just bought. To think this way takes mental practice. It means going against the current of what is accepted as normal. But it soon becomes something immensely rewarding. It's time we claimed back our personal pleasure in doing humble tasks well.

The Longing for a Ritual Space

Let's extend this discussion in a slightly different direction. We have a powerful yearning for a mythic world and a ritualized one, and it is expressed, strangely enough, through our love affairs with cars and kitchens. I suspect that if it were possible to calculate how many waking hours we spend in our cars and our kitchens we'd find we spend more time in those places than almost anywhere else. Let's take a moment to look at this. The modern car is a far different item from the earliest vehicles, where there was in every case a sense of the maker's hand in each aspect of the construction. Perhaps one even knew the name of the factory owner (Henry Ford, for example) and his personality was stamped on those rickety cars, each of which showed its mechanical improvements. Car owners were likely to talk about who had designed it, what materials were used, and how the motor worked. This was a machine, weighed down with the solidity of its construction process.

Today the modern car seems to hide its origins under the sleek and seamless forms that are all beginning to resemble each other. It's as if it had appeared, fully complete, from another planet. Even the advertisements tend to reinforce this. The most common ad is usually of a car zooming through an empty landscape—a desert, a salt flat, beautiful countryside with fjords and mountains, or even a preternaturally empty city, but as it happens, almost no homes, people, or other vehicles. The cars accelerate and turn skidding circles at high speed, and the countryside remains territory to be traversed fast rather than experienced. The overall sense is that once we buy a car, we are set free from the material world, weightless, free of humble needs, such as shopping in crowded malls, or ordinary experiences such as being stuck in rush-hour traffic.

Even the ads that show the car being produced tend to show spotless factories equipped with robots, and an absence of real people. Ford did, for a while, feature actors who said they were assembly workers, all looking unconvincingly clean and relaxed at their work, but that ad approach was discontinued due to soft sales. It seems we don't want to be reminded of the hard, dirty, physical labor that goes into these glorious machines. Occasionally we will have ads that show the car in a wind-tunnel, for example, where there is a sense of speed and even of flight, as the thin streams of smoke whip over the aerodynamic shape like clouds going past an airplane's wings. The car is hardly felt as a solid object on a road but as a flying miracle, elegant, other-worldly.

The ads obviously work, which tells us that people love the fantasyland of driving, of being in a luxuriously upholstered box, insulated from the outside world and its discomforts. Air conditioning, heated seats, adjustable seats, stereo, GPS, and video—most car interiors are more comfortable than the average living room. All this is, usually, for just one person: the driver.

Most drivers today are so remote from the mechanical workings of the car that they do not know with any certainty what sort of motor is in the car, nor do they care. They do not know where the sleek, semi-matte stainless steel fixtures come from or who put them there or what processes were required to make them. All they care about is whether they look good and feel good to the touch.

I'm not critical of this experience. I think it's delightful to be able to get into a car and not have to be assailed with its physical limitations, vibrations, and demands. Nothing much needs to be monitored except at high speed. It's travel without reference to the physical world. It's a journey that can be measured in the length of time it takes to get from A to B, rather than these many miles and this much gasoline.

All of which suggests that for many of us a car—the luxury car that we are encouraged to lust after—can offer a rarified experience that leaves us remote from the real world. It's a sort of out-of-body freedom from our normal limitations. It is, in one sense, a spiritual experience. I think that for many people the spiritual experience they long for, the mythic sense of being attached to a miraculous method of transport, like a winged horse, exists mostly in the car showrooms of the world.

What this shows us is that the hunger for a mythic experience has been hijacked and exploited by those who wish to sell us metal boxes that will self-destruct over time, while costing us a lot of money.

A slightly different phenomenon is the modern kitchen, which is not just a place for the efficient preparation of food but a temple to the gods of beauty. The faucets, the sinks, the appliances, the cabinets—all are available, if one has the money, in the form of sculptural objects: cool, smooth, and elegant. The granite countertops, the variety of floor surfaces, such as rustic terra cotta Saltillo tiles that remind us of the farmhouse that this kitchen was never even close to—all these are remote from actual cooking. Instead, they are statements about beauty, harmony, and something very static. The elegant kitchen is not really to be used for gutting and filleting a haul of fish, for instance, or to be cluttered with pans, as a real cook comes to grips with a complex recipe. Instead the kitchen is a haven of peace and order, of quiet and elegance, where a small salad appears miraculously alongside a glass of perfectly chilled white wine, in a moment of soft lighting, and possibly of romance.

This is a long way from a real kitchen as experienced by most people, where the space has pans in use or waiting to be washed, food stacked ready to be used, or wastes that need to be thrown out. In the perfect fashionable kitchen, there are no stray papers, no odd bills that get pushed behind the fruit tray, no bits of casual kitchen detritus.

In the case of both the kitchen and the car, we are looking into a perfected, simplified world of peace and beauty. And the question I'd ask is this: Why do we want peace and beauty in our most active areas of life, our cars and our kitchens? Those are places that should, by rights, be a bit chaotic and rough around the edges; yet, it is exactly because they are not usually peaceful that the advertisers want us to experience them that way. We look at our lives and we say: Why isn't my kitchen like something out of a design magazine? Why isn't my car a gleaming miracle? Yet behind this is the real question: Why isn't there anything holy, calm, and beautiful in my life, where I can bask in the feeling of peace?

We buy cars and kitchens because we have to have them; but we also buy into an image of luxurious cars and refined kitchens that in actuality reflects our longing for a ritual space, a mythic experience. Unfortunately, we are looking for it in all the wrong places. Of course, holiness and calm are always helped by the existence of a quiet and meditative space. A church, synagogue, temple, or a grove of trees will offer that, but only if we have the ability to find peace within ourselves once we are there. In a car, we are unlikely to be at peace, since driving is not a particularly peaceful activity. It requires us to be alert to the outside world, rather than in harmony with the inner world. A kitchen is "the heart of the home" for some people; it is usually a social, noisy and active place, with a ringing phone and streams of people looking for food.

So we spend our money on a new car—perhaps $40,000 or more—and we purchase our new kitchen at perhaps twice that price, and we still don't get peace. We have, in fact, invested in the wrong ritual spaces.

So the crux of the problem is this: Our endless pursuit of diversions prevents us from getting what we want: inner peace. You don't have to spend a fortune on a kitchen or a car or on anything to get that. You simply need a calm "ritual space" as a backdrop so that you can find it within yourself. Inner peace doesn't require an elaborate ceremony, or any ceremony at all. You just need to have an open mind—one that wants to see the transcendent in all things. Then you simply allow for that urge to arise somewhere safe, somewhere away from the world's needs.

Claiming the Ritual Space

Finding transcendent, calm, ritual spaces that work for us as individuals requires us to be awake to the opportunities that life sends us. Here's Edward Thomas's poem "Adlestrop" to show what I mean. It's about a train ride, when the steam locomotive pauses at an out-of-the-way station in England one summer day, in 1914, on the eve of World War One. The poet looks out of the window and is unimpressed at first, since all he sees is the station's name sign:

> Yes. I remember Adlestrop—
> The name, because one afternoon
> Of heat the express-train drew up there
> Unwontedly. It was late June.
>
> The steam hissed. Someone cleared his throat.
> No one left and no one came
> On the bare platform. What I saw
> Was Adlestrop—only the name
>
> And willows, willow-herb, and grass,
> And meadowsweet, and haycocks dry,
> No whit less still and lonely fair
> Than the high cloudlets in the sky.
>
> And for that minute a blackbird sang
> Close by, and round him, mistier,
> Farther and farther, all the birds
> Of Oxfordshire and Gloucestershire.[1]

It's a remarkable poem because it's so simple, and because that blackbird singing in the tree transports him to a sense of the vastness of this ancient, eternal landscape. Instead of being cocooned in his railway carriage's compartment, behind the glass, in his own thoughts, perhaps impatient of delay, the poet feels the eternal spaces open up around him. He is in contact with the power of the seasons, with nature, and sees his place in it. It's a moment worthy of the Buddha. We are in this world, yet we are eternal; and the connection between the two is beauty. Any place can be a ritual place if it allows us to do that.

The poem was first published in 1917. Since the First World War, in which Thomas was killed, was well under way at this time, his memory of a peaceful railway ride in June 1914 is all the more poignant. Thomas, recalling the event, gives us a moment of holiness.

An earlier poet, William Wordsworth, referred to this sort of experience as encountering "spots of time," as if he'd temporarily stepped into another dimension of awareness.

The German poet Rilke describes a similar moment of deep recognition of the power that is in the earth and heavens, in roughly the same way: The poem is called "The Wait":

> It's a train that suddenly stops
> With no station around,
> And we can hear the cricket,
> And, leaning out the carriage door,
>
> We vainly contemplate
> A wind we feel that stirs
> The blooming meadows, the meadows
> Made imaginary by this stop.[2]

Each poet describes moments that are transcendent, if we can be alert to them. Anything can become a ritual space if we are awake.

I'll spell it out: We cannot be alert to these moments unless we know they're worth paying attention to. That doesn't come just by chance but by training, practice. Ritual can train us to become more sensitive to possibility all around us. Like a bird watcher, who gazes at the heavens alert to what may wing by, we'll be able to identify what comes our way as an eagle or a lark if we've paid attention beforehand. If we haven't, then the bird will just be a shape randomly flying by, and we won't know how to respond. And so the value will be lost.

In my writing workshops and my individual work with writers, as a first step I ask them to claim a space that they will use only for writing, and only at certain times of day. It might be as simple as appropriating one side of a dining table, every day, for 10 minutes, then turning up to write each day. Without this commitment to claiming a personal ritual space in which the writer can go inward, it is almost impossible for most people to keep up a writing practice. Without the space, without the ritual, it is very much harder to find what it is one has to say.

CHAPTER TWENTY-FIVE

A Theory of Ritual and Myth: Choosing the Way Forward

We can now begin to construct a general schema of how myth and ritual work within our society, and to do so we'll need to adapt some ideas from Roland Barthes. Barthes' book *Mythologies* proved important in the 1950s for generating ideas about modern myths. He was interested in other fields than those we have been discussing here, but those of you who know his work will notice some echoes, I've no doubt.

If we look at the rituals and myths we've been discussing and ask how they fit together, what we can begin to construct is a five-stage structure where meanings are added to larger meanings to arrive at myth.

Take the idea of Christmas, for example. There are various actions associated with it. Decorating a tree is simply an action without any prejudices. If it's done in May, it probably has only a personal significance, a different "value," and possibly could be assumed by some to be critical of the existing social custom. But a tree decorated around the end of December suddenly assumes all sorts of expectations. It "should" be an evergreen, according to most customs, but the actual form of decoration is pretty wide open. So we have an act (tree decoration) that gathers meaning from the time and place it is done.

The Five Stages of Myth

Consider these aspects of Christmas now, as a series of stages. When we add an action like tree decoration (Stage 1) to the social situation of December 25th we have nothing more than a conventional result (Stage 2). Anyone can do this, no matter what religious beliefs or disbeliefs one has. A shopkeeper can put a decorated tree in a window simply to attract customers.

But if this action at Stage 2 is associated with accompanying emotions—wonder, delight, a sense of reverence—then we reach Stage 3: The action becomes a ritual. Now this ritual can be as personal and as idiosyncratic as you wish, but once an emotion is part of the activity, it becomes an event that has added power for at least some of those involved.

Once an event has this ritual aspect, once the emotions are involved, then the event itself can become linked with other events. In the case of Christmas and Christmas trees, which is the example we've chosen for the moment, the whole process of decorating the tree can be associated with the historical value of Christmas. At this point the presents placed under the tree remind people, perhaps, of the three kings bearing gifts, and the evergreen tree reflects on the undying value of religious beliefs. This adds meaning to the ritual and deepens the experience, especially for those who accept that form of religious expression. When that happens, we have a series of stories that circle around the ritual, providing a context that goes beyond the immediate lives of those involved. This is Stage 4.

At this point, some people may see the pagan roots of the worship of an evergreen tree during the depths of winter, and others may see the lights on the tree as symbolic of the light Jesus brought into the world, and so on. This is when we have a mythology that is not specifically about the tree, but of which the tree is a reminder. Stories collect around the tree. This is the richness of myth, any myth. It links us to a larger set of human spiritual values. This is Stage 5 of the sequence.

Notice, the tree functions this way no matter how big or small or fine or ugly it is. The tree itself seems to fade behind its larger significance as a "Christmas Tree."

The stages can be sketched out, then, as follows;

1. The neutral fact;
2. The fact seen in a local context of meanings;
3. The emotions that collect around stages 1 and 2 cause this to become a **RITUAL** action;
4. The ritual is now seen as part of a larger historical context;
5. Stages 3 and 4 combine to provide a series of stories and beliefs that can be called a **MYTH**, reaching Stage 5.

Some of the myths we've been looking at function this way, but many of them stall half way through, when they are still rituals.

Let's spell this out by referring back to an example of a ritual we have today that loses energy, that stalls before it can gain its full power. I'll put numbers in parentheses after each stage, to guide you through.

The driving permit test is a fact (Stage 1), and it is usually linked to the birthday closest to which one can get the permit (Stage 2). So the exam and an individual's 16th birthday are linked. Some emotions do come to the surface around this event, but they are on the whole shallow and the "ritual" is only talked about for a short time afterward (Stage 3). What very often happens at this point is that the ritual stalls. It has nowhere else to go. No one really wants to talk much about driving tests beyond a certain point.

If we were to extend the ritual and make it the starting point of an ongoing series of discussions in which we talked further about the nature of responsibility, safety, and personal duty, then we would be able to link this event to a wider series of considerations (Stage 4). At that point we would be positioning the young person's experience in history. Then we would be creating a mythology of some effectiveness about what it means to be a responsible citizen (Stage 5).

I use this example in part because one of my workshop participants described how she, with a new driver's permit at age 16, nearly knocked down a motorcyclist, and how the angry motorcyclist forced her car to stop and dragged her out of the car to yell at her. In the ensuing shouting match the motorcyclist, also a woman, punched her in the face and broke her nose. The case eventually went to court and took months to resolve. At the end of that time, the young woman reported, "I really knew a lot about safety, responsibility, and the fragility of human life!"

Can you see the difference? The ritual, which had stalled before it could take on any mythic value, was forcibly jumpstarted. The emotions attached to this lesson became real, powerful, and memorable. The lesson was learned, where previously it had been barely noticed. Lives were saved as a result. The method was hardly the best, but its effectiveness cannot be denied.

Now, let's look at a different example. In the case of a topic like gun ownership we can do a similar analysis, and we'll find a slightly surprising outcome.

Owning a gun is a fact, which is legally permitted (Stage 1). If we place it in context, though, we'll notice that there are no hostile Indians, few wild animals to threaten us or provide essential food, and plenty of police to help us if we need help (Stage 2). So gun ownership is now a specific choice rather than an absolute necessity. This choice has to do, perhaps, with the new owner feeling empowered, self-sufficient, and safe from threat—even if those threats are ill defined. So buying a gun has an emotional resonance that makes it into a ritual act that says, "I am a person who thinks this way and believes this to be the state of the world" (Stage 3).

The point here is that there is considerable rhetoric around gun ownership in the United States, with the National Rifle Association (NRA) and others freely spreading their own ideas about what it "means" to own a gun. They provide the historical context required for Stage 4 by dazzling us with stories about the American War of Independence and the sacred nature of the United States Constitution and our freedoms. All this, added together, has emotional resonance that speaks us of "the American way"—even if we no longer need to fight for independence from Britain. And so the story becomes a cherished myth about what makes us American and different from other nations. The story has achieved Stage 5, where the gun is now part of a whole system of belief. It has achieved mythic status.

Make no mistake, this is a powerful myth. Unfortunately, it also has a few logical flaws. It doesn't, for example, take note of the problems of gang-related deaths, drug shootouts, and children as casualties of this policy. It's a myth that is based on a questionable premise: that the world around us is unsafe in a very specific way and that guns are the answer. Two centuries ago that made sense; today, it may not.

Just to remind you: In the United States, some 12,000 people die each year in hand-gun–related incidents (I can't call them accidents, although some are). That's three times as many Americans as died in the second Iraq War, which lasted the best part of a decade, all told. That historical fact is rarely applied to the mythic structure so many people buy into. If it were to be included at Stage 4, perhaps we'd have a different outcome.

The Connection between Myth and Therapy

In case these five stages of ritual and myth seem somewhat remote from real, lived experience, I'd point out that what is happening is exactly the same as what occurs in modern psychology when we look at the deeper meanings behind a person's actions.

Here's another way of looking at it. A red sports car is a fact (Stage 1). But a red sports car, purchased by a middle-aged man, takes on a specific meaning (Stage 2). When the emotions felt by the new owner are added to the mix we have a ritual action that says, "I'm having some midlife thoughts about who I am." This is Stage 3. If we add that information to what we know about the status of middle-aged men in our society—how they feel disregarded, unattractive, and ineffective compared to younger men and how there is a sudden spike in suicide levels for men at this time of life—then we have an historical context to begin to help us assess this behavior (Stage 4). At that point we can create a full-blown story, a myth we can all identify, called "the midlife crisis" (Stage 5). This process of decoding is exactly what the psychologist and the therapist do. They observe behaviors in order to find the deep unconscious story, or myth, that the individual is living out.

Ideally the therapist will be able to disentangle the myth from the reality and perhaps advise the middle-aged man about how he can get the recognition he longs for in a more direct way. This is a simple example, but its validity suggests that myth creation is fundamentally part of who we are, and that understanding it can be truly beneficial. We are myth-creating creatures at every level, and sometimes we need help to disentangle the myths we create.

Choosing Myths

If we can see how myths work, whether they be good or bad, then we can begin to identify which ones seem to enhance life and which seem to lead toward destruction.

This is important. As I touched on earlier in this book, the Nazis famously created a mythology that worked to demonize segments of society they deemed inconvenient, and they created this new mythology exactly according to the precepts we have been examining. Let's now take a closer look at some of the mythologies they constructed to boost their own status.

These myths were based around 19th-century composer Richard Wagner's music, old folk tales, and Aryan beliefs. The beliefs were distorted along the precise lines we've been considering. A blue-eyed blonde haired boy is simply a fact (Stage 1). Such a boy singing a rousing patriotic folk song in a mountain landscape is a figure placed in a staged context (Stage 2), one that is guaranteed to create an emotional response. So the combination of fact and the circumstance creates a ritualized scene with an overt message: We must all revere the activity of singing patriotic songs in a landscape, preferably surrounded by Nordic type companions (Stage 3). This is "good," is what it says. When this image is projected on a movie screen, with loud music, it is blended into a larger discourse about what it means to be "German," and other pseudo-historical discussions (Stage 4). The movie audience is encouraged to sing along to the patriotic song, and soon enough we have a full-blown myth, a series of values that most people present are ready to accept (Stage 5).

In deconstructing this Nazi-manufactured myth, the weakest link is the evocation of what it means to be "German," of course. "German" is an artificial construct, every bit as elusive and contradictory and impossible to define as "American" or "British" or "Senegalese." The success of the Nazi propaganda machine depended on manipulating this idea to suit its own ends. Uniforms, or uniform-like clothes—think of those young men and women depicted in "traditional" national costumes—help in this instance, and the fascist regimes of all nations have always been keen on uniforms that help us not to see individuals but merely "representatives" or "types." The uniforms flatten the human richness to a mere cipher, and the concept of what is "German" is made deceptively easy to swallow.

Healthy mythology does not seek to close off discussion in this way; it always seeks to open up the topic for examination.

Looking back at the myth of Icarus and the wings made of wax and feathers, for example, we can see that the myth does not seek simply to blame the young man for being irresponsible. We could see it that way, of course, but that would be a limited way of looking at the story. Instead, the story asks questions about the personal cost to the father, to Daedalus, of not allowing himself time to think through what his new invention might mean for the next generation. The cost is his son, and with that loss his family's lineage. In prison, the two of them had no future, but in seeking an escape and a new future using too rash a means they destroy any possible future.

In our world of new inventions every week we would be well advised if we were to bear that in mind. Products are released every day, and we have no idea what their long-term effects may be. This is true of medical drugs, computer games, and so much more. The "irresponsibility" motif exists for father *and* son, when we look at it with open eyes. This story invites us into a more open mythic discussion, which is why it is valuable.

Myth creation, as we've seen, is a normal and natural aspect of human thinking. What we've been at pains to reveal is how the process works and how we can be alert to its many forms. When we know how it works we can choose the most suitable myths and discard those that are unhelpful or destructive. When we see that myth creation is truly about getting in touch with our deep sense of what is holy in our lives, then we can reclaim the holiness, without confusion or doubt, and reestablish the vital connection with the earth that we so deeply desire. Failing to do this will lead us ever deeper into alienation from ourselves and our relationship to this planet, and eventually it will hasten our destruction.

If we continue to accept passively whatever stories the world of advertising tells us about ourselves, if we swallow these plausible half-truths and ignore our own internal needs, then we will live half lives, and not full, truly present lives. Our rituals will become whatever the commercials tell us they should be. In this way the world of consumerism offers a mythology every bit as unsustainable as any other piece of contrived propaganda. The difference is that now we know it. Now we can claim back our authentic spiritual lives.

Metaphor and Myth

In these pages I've been at pains to show that ritual, which is one way of feeding spiritual hunger, is varied and resonant and profoundly human. It also depends upon an awareness of metaphor. In metaphor one describes something in terms of something else. So, "He eats like a horse" refers to the amount the person eats, not that he eats only oats and hay and grass. It is suggestive of the person's manner, not prescriptive.

Now, let's apply this to the opening of the Bible, where we are told that God created man in his image. It's a specifically religious reference, so it has particular resonance here. If we take this idea literally we'll have the assumption that God looks just like us. After all, that's what it says. So it makes sense to have a powerful older man with a white flowing beard as the image of God on the Sistine Chapel ceiling. This notion runs into trouble, though, when we have black African congregations gazing upon the image of a white Anglo-Saxon who looks nothing like them. It also leaves out the tricky question of how women fit into the equation. If we were to take this literal approach and consider it critically, what would we come up with? For one thing, we'd have to conclude that Man cannot be formed directly in God's image because there are so many versions of what humans can look like that we'd have no stable image to hang on to. We can look like seven-foot-tall basketball players in Detroit and starving children in China, and any number of variations on the theme.

It's much more helpful, though, if we take this idea that Man was made in God's image and see that what may be intended is a notion that all of us, every single last one of us, reflects God in some way. We are all part of God's work; we all are the faces of God. If we accept this, we have a radically different idea of what's going on, one that comes closer to "love your enemies" than anything else in its acceptance of the divine nature that exists in all people.

Interestingly enough this rather sophisticated idea exists in such rituals as the hospitality given by Muslims to strangers they may meet, whom they are obliged to welcome and take care of, at least at the beginning. The saying is that the guest should be welcome, for this may be a messenger of Allah in disguise. Obviously, we can see this as religious doctrine, or superstition, or as tribal custom, and dismiss it as quaint. Or we can see that behind the ritual is the hint, the ghost, of a way of responding to others that is profoundly spiritual, one that sees God in every face, everywhere. That is very appealing. It's also directly in opposition to what the Catholic Church has been saying for a long time—that God is not inside each of us but outside us, and has to be invited in.

The primary urge in this particular ritual is, arguably, one of acceptance and love. Political structures have altered its value, and even attempted to overturn its worth, leaving our spiritual hunger unmet. It's our task to get back to the center of our rituals, to disentangle them from the misuse they've suffered, and to start living their spiritual values again.

Let us never forget that our essential link is to eternity. It is to the majesty of the heavens and the sense that we are all connected, through our hearts, in love and understanding. We are not separate. Ritual will help us see this, so that we can perceive what it is the universe needs each of us to do. The shiny toys placed so seductively in front of us by those who wish us to follow the path of the ego will only lead us toward discontent, obsession, and isolation. Fortunately, we have ritual and myth to remind us that there is another way.

CHAPTER TWENTY-SIX

Ritual is the Activity
That Makes Us Human:
A Primary Structure
of the Psyche

This discussion of myth and ritual and their impact on us in our daily lives would not be complete without asking whether this is not, perhaps, just something we human beings use to confuse or delude ourselves. The only answer we can definitely give is that myth and ritual have been used for countless generations, since long before written language, to help us explain our situation as finite beings in an infinite universe. In each case the myth or ritual helps us explore the world to which we are linked in ways that are mysterious.

More than this, though, is the sense we have that we may be the only creatures on earth that feel this so acutely. Certain animals seem to be aware of this temporal/eternal opposition in their lives, but we cannot say for sure how they feel it. Humans are the only creatures we know of who actively suffer and fail to thrive if the belief structures within which we live are not strong.

To look for more insight we must move into a realm of speculation, and perhaps an unusual one. In 1994, a cave system was discovered in France, inside which were found the oldest cave paintings yet known. Named "The Cave of Forgotten Dreams," its walls are covered with bold, beautiful, reverently drawn images of bison, horses, and bulls from 30,000 years ago. Werner Herzog, the German filmmaker, gained permission to film these images in 2011, so the paintings are once more available for public viewing. When interviewed, Herzog made some interesting comments, which I think bear repeating here. He pointed out that these paintings were highly accomplished, done in a spirit of love rather than, say, hate. This was obviously not just a depiction of food waiting to be slaughtered.

150

He then pointed out that these were drawn not by Neanderthal man, but by *homo sapiens*, the species of hominid from which we are descended. Neanderthal man, a highly successful species, had no sense of art or decoration, as far as we know. Neanderthal sites have so far yielded no signs of creative activities aside from tool and weapon making, while *homo sapiens* seems to have had, at the same time in history, impressive artistic abilities, as seen in the cave paintings. And perhaps *homo sapiens* also had a sense of mysticism, reflected in the placing of these images deep within caves. By candle or torch light they would have swum into view, as surprising as images encountered in dreams. In addition *homo sapiens* has left fragments of what appear to be bone flutes, for making music, presumably.

Herzog says, in a way that an archaeologist might be reluctant to suggest, that what makes us human, what makes us who we are and not Neanderthals, is the ability to create images and music, where one thing stands for another. The images in the caves are, surely, about the wonder of life, and how we are part of it and yet observers of it at the same time, slightly apart. I do not think this is simply a projection of our values upon those paintings.

This supposition, which feels true even if it cannot be proven yet, tells us at least one important truth. What makes us distinctively human is our ability to think figuratively, to create stories, myths, and rituals that evoke a sense of wonder. It is the basis of all that we are as a species. When we deny this ability we deny, in effect, what makes us human. Our present-day spiritual hunger is testimony that we long for just such a close and deep experience of the ritual and mythic elements in our lives. This may at first seem like a problem, but it is in fact a signpost that points to the solution, telling us what we need to do for ourselves.

And that is exactly why I wrote this book—to remind us of what makes us human, so that we can continue to be the best version of ourselves, living in reverence with our past, with compassion for our fellow creatures, and looking forward to all that the future will ask of us.

PART VII

Conclusion

CHAPTER TWENTY-SEVEN

What it all Means:
Myth and Ritual and
the Six Archetypes

All of the rituals we've considered have been actions—actions designed to remind individuals about who they are and where they came from and, often, about what they must remember about themselves in times of crisis. Most of these have also been socially recognized rituals, upheld by the groups that use them. I've included some private ritualized behaviors of individuals, because individual moments can, of course, be recalled as important in the same way as more public occasions.

Ultimately these private moments have the same overall function: establishing a sense of identity as the individual moves through life. These are moments when we know something has changed.

What we don't yet have is a strong central narrative that ties all these rituals together, so we can say with certainty: This is what all these things are about, and this is where they lead us. In this final chapter, we're now going to make these important connections.

We couldn't do this earlier. The time we've spent examining rituals and myths has been in the service of finding out which of them are nurturing, life-giving actions, and which are not. We're now going to focus on the authentic rituals. Up until this point, we have not been able to come to a clear sense of what it all means because we've had to face a mixture of spirit-centered rituals and commercially promoted quasi-rituals. In this section what we'll see is that each of those healthy rituals, each of these ways of dealing effectively with our spiritual hunger, seems to be a fragment of a coherent larger belief system.

Think of the ritual events we've examined here as a series of buoys, bobbing on the surface of the sea. From where we stand we can see the colored buoys but not the nets strung between them below the surface, the nets that connect them and will pro-

154

duce the harvest of the deep sea. That underlying web exists, and links all these ritual actions, stories, and legends. If we can understand this we can revalue rituals and see why they have so much value for us even today.

So what is the connection? What is the system?

It has to do specifically with what I have written about archetypes, in my other books: *Stories We Need to Know* (Findhorn Press, 2008) and *The Six Archetypes of Love* (Findhorn Press, 2008). The point is this: *Each authentic ritual we have looked at is an enactment of a psychic awareness, linked to a specific archetypal stage of development; each is an echo of the six central archetypes that span Western culture.*

Those six archetypes—**INNOCENT, ORPHAN, PILGRIM, WARRIOR-LOVER, MONARCH, MAGICIAN**—are the true underpinnings of these ritual actions. They exist throughout 3,000 years of the Western world's literature and myth: always the same six, always in the same order, and always concerned with the same issues. From Homer to Harry Potter, through Sophocles, Euripides, Shakespeare, Dante, the Bible, the Nineteenth Century novelists, and up to the present day, they are always present, always recognizably the same.

This has been made clear in my earlier studies, where these six archetypes are seen as visual images depicting the developmental stages we are all invited to go through, if we wish, and the stages are mirrored in the great literature of every age. Literature, myth, legend, and ritual have always been tools to teach us about how we can grow to full adulthood. Of course, we can also refuse to rise to this challenge, but such a choice would ensure a particular type of psychological stasis, one that ritual urges us to question each time we encounter it. This is because rituals are always about marking points of change.

For those who are unfamiliar with my earlier writing, let me give a brief overview of the six archetypes and how they work.

We all start off as **INNOCENTS**, whether it's when we're born or, later, when we face the first day at a new job and temporarily slip back into this way of being. To some extent, we're all Innocents whenever we fall in love—at least for a while. Perhaps we trust too readily, or forgive too quickly, because that is what the Innocent is truly good at: trusting and loving. They're important attributes, since no adult relationship can last long without trust and love, but it's also a dangerous way to be.

We quickly learn that life isn't easy and not everyone can be trusted, so at this point we look for a protector, someone we can learn from, or just a fellow-sufferer we can latch on to for now. Just as children clump together in a playground because any friend is better than no friend, so adults can join an organization, a club, a clique, or a gang, just to fit in and get along according to the rules. Many will take on unsatisfactory relationships and stay in them, because a bad relationship still seems better than being alone. This is how many of us agree to become **ORPHANS**, adopted into the existing powerful social systems, which then give us recognizable status. Unfortunately this comes at a cost, since in order to conform we must give up our individuality to some extent.

Some people are not content to fit in for very long, though, and they become questioners, outcasts, or seekers after their personal truth. They become **PILGRIMS**. This can be a restless and difficult time, and if we want a present-day image of the Pilgrim it might be the teenager who doesn't know what she wants, but knows with great clarity what she *doesn't* want. The rebels of this world start off as Pilgrims, better at rejecting than at constructing.

When Pilgrims find the person or people they wish to be with and the life task they wish to devote themselves to, they take a big step. They become **WARRIOR-LOVERS**, ready to make a stand peacefully for what they believe in. Some may even die for their cause. This archetype can manifest itself in the role of the passionate revolutionary, working peacefully for change, or in the role of the quiet reformer, standing up for what is decent and right. The all-important shift is that Warrior-Lovers recognize that the life task is more important than they are. Ask any parent who has sacrificed to make sure his or her children get what they need, and you'll see what I mean.

Warrior-Lovers will, eventually, recognize that life is not a one-person crusade and will set themselves the task of training others in what they know. At that point, they can become **MONARCHS**, nurturing not just their nearest and dearest, but anyone who seems to be worthy of the task. Doing this takes skill, humility, courage, and trust. Ask any teacher who is any good at the job.

The Monarch is not just a manager, though. At a certain point, the Monarch archetype has to let go of control and begin to encourage people to take charge of their own lives, to be the best version of themselves they can be, whatever form that takes. And when that happens people discover more courage, more devotion, and more strength than they ever believed possible. And that's the magic. **THE MAGICIAN** makes it happen in others.

This bears directly on everything we've been discussing.

Obviously we can't all become world leaders, which is perhaps the highest version of the Magician. Yet we can, in our personal lives and in our professional lives, be the best parents, friends, supporters, and community contributors we are capable of being. Each role is vital, because it helps to cause positive change. At times we're all capable of being Magicians in the ways we can inspire others, or change their negative energies to positive ones. The three realms—the personal, the communal, and the political—all need our attention, and all need to be balanced. It is just as important to deal in a fair and loving way with our family as it is to be respectful of our next-door neighbor, for if we can't do that it will be very hard for any of us to treat other countries fairly.

How does this apply to rituals? The rituals we've looked at are the social reminders of the existence of these six archetypes, and what they require of us.

So, let's be specific. The Innocent, the first of the six archetypes, is commemorated in religious events like baptisms, circumcisions, and so on, and also in all those pictures we see of the Madonna and Child in churches and cathedrals. Christmas is a celebration of the Innocent, of the new hope and new birth—and a new year. As any new parent knows, the arrival of a baby changes everything. It puts us in contact with the wonder of the Innocent, and also the responsibility of caring for this fragile new creature, as we saw in Chapter Eleven. We're reminded of this important series of truths every year at Christmas, whether or not we have children. In a slightly different way this archetype is honored in British artist Anthony Gormley's sculpture "Waste Man" and similar ritual performance art events we looked at in Chapter Fourteen, since the burning away of the past and everything that keeps us stuck allows for a clean start, a rebirth.

The Orphan archetype is present in First Communions and Confirmations, where the individual is declared to be part of a specific religion. At this point, the young person is basically agreeing to join a belief system, as an Orphan ready to be "adopted" into the accepted power structure. The candidate for Confirmation, or First Communion, or Bar/Bat Mitzvah, is told what to believe and think, so this is not yet an individual belief system for him or her. But it's worth noticing that this type of event is also mirrored in our education system as a whole, where transition to High School involves crossing a boundary, one that asks the students to abide by a series of rules in exactly the same way as the religious ceremonies do. If we think back to the experiences I described at the start of this book in Chapter Two, when I was sent to boarding school, I arrived there as a lost Orphan, and joined a shifting set of loyalties that had to do with who was acceptable and who was not. This is the territory of the Orphan in one of its grimmer forms.

Many rituals are designed to keep people acquiescent and docile, of course, cushioned in the Orphan's situation. Yet we've also seen that ritual hurdles, such as driving tests, drinking ages, graduations, and so on, are a way in which the young person tests and acknowledges the limits of what is acceptable.

This is the Pilgrim archetype in action, as each person seeks to decide who he or she is by going beyond the boundaries. This used to be expressed in the ritual of taking a year off before or after college (a Gap Year) to "find oneself," and it has since become part of the unexpressed curriculum in most American colleges. Today, many students go to college not so much to study as to leave home, sow some wild oats and, perhaps, grow up. Either way, it is still seen as a developmental milepost, a phase, and the social response has been to incorporate this human need into a ritualized social structure, called a Bachelor's Degree.

In Chapter Three, you may recall I described my parachute jumps, and how they gave me a sense of the wonder and fragility of being alive. This experience, in archetypal terms, was that of the Pilgrim, the risk-taker who pushes to the edges just to find out where the edges are. In the process, the Pilgrim can learn a great deal about who he or she is. Religious pilgrims, even today, go on long treks to holy shrines, praying and exploring their relationship to their god on the way. Their hope is to come to greater clarity about themselves as they travel to the shrine, whether it be to Mecca, Benares, or to the great European cathedrals. The actions are varied, but the meanings are the same.

Only when the young person knows who he or she is—and perhaps that takes many similar Pilgrim experiences—can we expect him or her to form a deep bond with another person and find a way back into society. An example of this might be what happens when young people take their wedding vows, thereby implicitly agreeing to move into the Warrior-Lover archetype. The Warrior-Lover is the balance of stereotypical "male" power and "female" gentleness. Each person in a relationship must find that balance within themselves, and not rely on the other person to take on the missing role. Whenever that happens we tend to get a cliché, usually of the stern father and the indulgent mother, and real parenting doesn't happen. The marriage ceremony is what remains today to mark this transition, although once it had even deeper resonance as a declaration of Warrior-Lover status.

This balancing of male and female energies is what we see reflected in such strange ways in the ritual of the bullfight, which we discussed in Chapter Eight. The matador is dressed in ways that make him seem less than masculine, yet he demonstrates the courage of the soldier and the grace of a ballet artiste. He is a version of the Warrior-Lover, killing according to prescribed ideals, calm in the face of the bull's anger. The formalization of the activity has warped the archetype, but it also allows us to glimpse the origins of this strange sport as the enactment of the Warrior-Lover archetype. Certainly the action is cruel, but if we compare the killing in the bullring to what must have preceded it historically—a scrambled hunt in which men and dogs and bulls would be hacked to pieces—the bullfight is by comparison rather refined.

It's an image that appears in other places, also. In countless museums and churches, the image of St. George killing the dragon is not that far away from the imagery of the bullfight. These powerful icons hold clues as to what is happening beneath the surface. St. George rescuing the Virgin is a pretty clear depiction of the male and female aspects of the psyche moving toward union and balance. The Knight's strength is used in a worthy cause, and the fertile Virgin is now free to marry and produce children. The Warrior and the Lover fuse, and creativity is the result.

Our newspapers were full of similar images of the Warrior-Lover a few years back, when the United States first invaded Iraq. A favorite scene, which was repeated at various times, was of soldiers in battle gear comforting crying Iraqi babies or giving candy to young children. The soldier, who is after all a skilled killer, was presented as having compassion and a heart. Today, that image has been replaced by one that shows soldiers returning home, hugging their wives and children. This, too, is an image of the Warrior who is also the Lover, the upholder of compassionate values. The archetype is being honored.

Now, no matter what we think about bullfighting, it is still far preferable to the practices of some cultures in which warfare and gun-ownership are the accepted ways for a man to become a man. We have already looked at this issue in Chapter Ten. There is a time in life to come to terms with death, but warfare seems to be effective mostly in traumatizing people and rendering them unfit for reintegration into the world. Those soldiers hugging their loved ones have an alarming incidence of post-traumatic stress disorder (PTSD), a distressing condition where the primitive adrenaline fight-or-flight response in the body perceives danger and overreacts even in ordinary nonthreatening situations. PTSD ultimately can split up families and destroy peace-time lives.

Clearly, the image of the Warrior-Lover is still persuasive. As a culture we seem to need it, and yearn for it, and so we are willing to look past the unfortunate realities behind it. Sadly, I cannot help feeling we have lost sight of the real human drama by accepting what amounts to propaganda, a distorted form of the archetype used, often, for debased political or recruiting purposes.

I grew up in a military family and trained as a cadet, so I have the utmost respect for the military. What I can't respect is the way healthy archetypes have been co-opted to perpetrate an untruth. The point I'm making is this: If we are not intimately acquainted with the full worth of rituals and the archetypes to which they refer, the rituals may be manipulated, distorted, and used against our best interests.

You may recall the description I gave of the funeral and burial rituals, and how psychologically consoling they can be. This facing of death is an important milestone for anyone, and it is truly at the heart of what the Warrior-Lover must face before he or she can transition to the next archetype. We all have to come to terms with death, loss, and our own mortality. We can do this without warfare.

When we looked at the Siena Palio, the horse race described in Chapter Nine, we saw another dimension of this issue. The value of that race was, in part, that the competing sections would have to come to terms with not succeeding, despite all their efforts. This profoundly human lesson, that the best man does not always win and that fate may have other plans for us, is an essential moral point for us all, and especially for the Warrior-Lover. The Warrior-Lover is going to be tempted by pride. The lesson is simple. None of us can hope to win every time. Perhaps we won't win even once. But that doesn't mean the race is not worth running.

The Monarch archetype appears when the Warrior-Lover takes the skills of executive coolness and nurturing love, matches them to a sense of humility, and begins to apply his or her awareness to the community. Warrior-Lovers do this knowing that they are working for the good of all and for the next generation—not for their own self-glorification. This is why the encounter with death is so important. It keeps even the proudest leader humble.

The leader who can be compassionate, yet take the burden of responsibility for hard decisions, is agreeing to become a Monarch. We witness this on a regular basis. Every election season, we hope our candidates will be both compassionate and decisive, and that is what they try to project. Yet, so often, within days of election, they become mere weathercocks, following whatever populist wind prevails. We know what we want from them, but we just don't seem to get it.

The Monarch archetype is what we hope for, and we desire it so much that this expectation is actually written into the electoral process. Part of the ritual of Presidential inaugurations is to have the newly elected person swear on a Bible to do the best he can for the country, "So help me God." He is, by these words, recognizing that he is the servant of a higher moral power, to whom he is answerable. Unfortunately, we have had several presidents who have not seemed to think themselves answerable to anyone or anything but their own vanity. The ritual has been so sadly debased, we see more of the longing for its fulfillment than anything else. But that longing tells us all we need to know about the value of the archetype.

A useful comparison is to be seen in the coins we carry. British and European coinage for centuries carried the monarch's name followed by "*Dei Gra*," short for *Dei Gratia*, or "By the Grace of God." The implication is clear: The monarch was there only as long as God thought it was a good idea, and the ruler was always expected to be answerable to the highest sense of morality.

That's a pretty good assessment of the true Monarch archetype. In contrast, when the Nazis took power they also took over God, and promptly made him subservient to their wishes. Their "*Gott Mit Uns*" on coins and on every soldier's belt-buckle meant "God is with Us." implying he's not with anyone else and he'll back them up because they're right. It's a shameless travesty of the Monarch archetype. In fact, the Nazi slogan is closer to a kind of school-yard assertion, a version of, "We've got my big brother in my gang!" These are the words of the Orphan archetype, trying to feel powerful, trying to feel like a Monarch. American coins carry the more neutral, and more thoughtful words: "In God We Trust." It's beautifully stated as a belief, an urging to do the right thing, aimed at both the rulers and the citizenry. It suggests that we are all to be held accountable for our personal decisions. It's just one more example that shows us how present and enduring the archetype of the Monarch still is. You see and hold those coins every day, after all.

What this tells us is that the true Monarch archetype knows how to do the right thing, no matter how hard it is, and also wishes to train the next generation so that after he or she dies there will be a meaningful successor. In our days of first-born sons inheriting family fortunes and then squandering them, this is evidently not such an easy task. The ideal Monarch is, in some ways, the protector of those rituals and values that will lead others forward. This is Moses, keeping the faith with God as he struggles through the desert leading his sometimes rebellious tribe. This is Jesus, instructing the disciples as to what they must do—the precise actions required of them are modeled at the Last Supper—knowing that they will all abandon him at Golgotha. But he also knows they'll come back later, stronger than ever. This is what Shakespeare wrote about in those of his plays that examined the problems of king-ship and rule—almost all of his plays, in fact.

We don't have many people of that caliber today. We only have a few university pro-fessors and idealists who take it upon themselves to teach real values, and show us how we can all become more humane individuals. Fortunately, they have strong ceremonials to support them. As we have seen, the graduation exercises at colleges model the way young people can be brought to a place of personal empowerment by those who are (we hope) Monarchs in their chosen field of expertise, nurturing the next generation.

Martin Luther King Jr., Nelson Mandela, Mohandas Gandhi—we don't need many such people to inspire us and transform us, for that is what the Magician does, the highest level of the archetypes. He or she moves us to become better than we ever thought we could be. Each of these leaders, and many others besides them, was able to reconnect with the peace and love and idealism of the Innocent archetype and mobilize those qualities in a meaningful way, as Magicians. Mother Teresa, the Dalai Lama, Desmond Tutu… the list could go on and on. Each of them knew what spiritual hunger was, and each of them knew that ritual could make a difference, but only if the ritual was connected to a deep sense of peaceful, loving, purpose. The results were astonishing. It was magic, by any other name. That's what we saw in the example of Nelson Mandela and the Springbok rugby team.

A more readily available image of the Magician might be the counselor, the priest, or the therapist, who can guide others' lives without ordering them around. Much of what happens in those transformative conversations may feel like a kind of ritual. The confidentiality of the office, the quiet time given just to the client's needs, the sermon in church or temple—all of these have aspects of ritual behaviors to them. If successful, the person who seeks guidance finds not just direction but strength within him- or herself that they did not know they had.

Again, we can look for a more obvious ritual: the Mass or the Communion, where the priest actually seems to perform an act of magic by transforming the bread into the body of Christ and the wine into the blood of Christ. Whether we believe this truly happens or not is, perhaps, beside the point. For what is being presented to us is the idea that we can change our way of seeing our world so that we can touch the eternal, and here is the person who regularly does that, the priest. It is a ritual that gestures directly to the Magician archetype, the power to transform the ordinary into the transcendent. Each time we see the beauty behind an ordinary action we are touched by this magic.

The important outcome from this is that we now have, if we so wish, a checklist that can allow us to assess ritual behaviors. Ask yourself, whenever you come across what feels like a ritual, how might it reflect the six archetypes?

INNOCENT: This archetype appears in any ritual in which a new beginning is welcomed, anything from a house-warming party to a baptism, or from a child's first music recital to the school play. All these occasions essentially validate the qualities of fresh, unjaundiced eyes, and we see the world anew, through the child's eyes.

ORPHAN: If the ritual you observe is one that emphasizes joining, sharing, and community, then it's most likely reinforcing the positive power of the Orphan. Think of any club gathering, and that includes everything from Cub Scouts to Seniors' bowling leagues. Think of sports games at any level as celebrations of the Orphan archetype, and you'll come to a new appreciation of Little League games and back-yard football.

PILGRIM: Similarly, a ritual that is about exploration and questioning, one that celebrates mischief and fun and doing things that question the accepted order—that's most likely to be a ritual that is expressing the qualities of the Pilgrim. That's April Fool's Day, or Carnival, or the Hindu holiday of Hooli. It's also true that any ritual that values more serious questioning is also likely to be linked to the Pilgrim. Every town has a library, and every library is a celebration of questioning.

WARRIOR-LOVER: The Warrior-Lover archetype's rituals are those that value the assuming of responsibility, especially of a shared kind, like marriage, as we have seen. When you see television footage of peaceful protesters for human rights, you're seeing the Warrior-Lover in one of its forms.

MONARCH: The Monarch appears in those rituals that stress taking charge or becoming a leader. Such rituals are less common, but they center around such events as individuals being sworn in to public office, and similar circumstances.

MAGICIAN: The Magician will be found wherever there are rituals that emphasize the transformation of energies to a higher level. Any art museum, with its valuing of the healing and transformative power of art, stands as a monument to this. And every city worth its salt has at least one of these.

This checklist is flexible, of course, but I think we can see how most rituals can fall easily under one heading only. We can also see that this progression is central to our lives. All healthy rituals are connected to one of the six archetypes.

In these pages we've seen that longings associated with spiritual hunger, which can be satisfied to some extent by ritual and legend, lead us toward the very center of some vital questions. How can we grow? And how we can reach real wisdom? Ritual can point us in the right direction, but one of the answers is to know—really know in our souls—about the six archetypes. Rituals always point to the archetypes that underpin them.

Previous generations had a good knowledge of this, because they saw the six stages reflected in every major piece of art and every story they encountered, as well as in the Bible and other holy books. Jesus's life story, in which he moved through all six archetypes, was widely known. Starting as an Innocent babe, (remember "the Massacre of the Innocents" decreed by King Herod?); living estranged from his parents as an Orphan, saying to them, "Know ye not that I must be about my father's business?"; making his Pilgrimage into the desert, and emerging as a fighter for peace, a Warrior-Lover—all this follows the form of the first four archetypes. At the crucifixion, where he was dubbed "The King of the Jews," Jesus took on the Monarch archetype, the one who holds himself responsible for everyone (although not quite in the way that people at the time expected); and finally, upon his subsequent resurrection, he proved himself as the Magician, the inspiration, since it is then that the disciples do, in fact, come into their own powers as the apostles. All this was so much part of the interior landscape of almost every Western citizen over the last twelve hundred years or so that they didn't need to spell it out as I have had to here.

The same story structure is also to be found in the stories of Moses and Mohammed. Moses, the Innocent in the bulrushes, becomes Moses the adopted Orphan. He then tests the limits of Egypt and eventually leaves, wandering like a Pilgrim in the desert. During this time he develops the skills of the Warrior-Lover, and when he is given the Ten Commandments he becomes a Monarch, setting down the law, upholding the spiritual values of the Jews. His final deed is to show the Israelites the Promised Land, whereupon he dies. And since he has been a charismatic leader his example lingers on for them all, working its Magic for the following generations. They aspire to follow his example.

The same six-stage progression is central to Islam, as well. Mohammed, the unlettered camel driver, leaves his home as an Orphan, goes on a Pilgrim's retreat to a cave, and hears the word of God. He emerges as a Warrior-Lover who rapidly becomes a leader, a Monarch preaching a moral code. His ability to inspire others, as a Magician, continues and grows even after his death. This is a six-part structure that seems to transcend religions.

In the East, the story of the Buddha's life follows the exact same pattern. The young prince Siddhartha is isolated from the world as an Innocent, behind the palace walls. One day he discovers pain and death and immediately feels estranged from all he once trusted. He knows, now, he is an Orphan. So, he escapes and goes looking for truth, a Pilgrim in the woods, seated beneath the Bodhi Tree. He undergoes temptations and emerges as a Warrior-Lover, firm in his beliefs. Then he takes on the role of a teacher, a Monarch. Finally, he shows the way to Enlightenment, as an inspiration to others, a Magician. We recognize the pattern, I'm sure.

Our forebears certainly weren't any better than we are. Their lives were harder, and many were illiterate and ignorant and even brutish. But society held itself together with ritual, story, and legend, appealing to the best parts of each member of the populace, even when wars and famines and plagues swept through the lands. And generally speaking, the social values remained intact despite the disasters. As a result, we in the West live in a time of unparalleled freedoms, respect, and decency. Ritual and myth helped to uphold and even to deepen the human values of our world. And at the center of this, underlying it all, was a deep intuitive sense of the concept of the six archetypes. That's what underpins these rituals, all the life-giving rituals we have considered.

Rituals are now fading from our society, and the awareness of the six archetypes is in danger of fading with them; and that is why so many of us are in a state of spiritual hunger and existential despair.

It may be time to get to know these archetypes, perhaps for the first time. They are the deep structures of the psyche, the primordial way we make meanings and direct our lives. They deserve to be understood. We owe it to ourselves.

Chapter 1

1. Sanyika Shakur AKA Monster Kody Scott. *Monster: The Autobiography of an L.A. Gang Member*. New York: Penguin, 1994, ch.1, p.12.

Chapter 2

1. Brene Brown was speaking at the TED talks, June 2010. See: *www.ted.com/talks/lang/eng/brene_brown_on_vulnerability.html*.
2. Center for Disease Control and Prevention: Government statistics dated 27 Oct. 2010. See: *http://www.cdc.gov/Motorvehiclesafety/Teen_Drivers/index.html*.
3. Initiation rites are described in many places, and I can only suggest here that the interested reader start with the superb *Rituals of Manhood: Initiation in Papua New Guinea*, Gilbert H. Herdt, ed. Berkeley, CA: University of California Press, 1982.
4. Edward Gibbon, *The History of the Decline and Fall of the Roman Empire*. London: T. Candell, Strand, 1837, ch. XV, p.189.

Chapter 4

1. Rumi. *The Essential Rumi*, trans. Coleman Barks. New York: Quality Paperback, 1995.

Part II

1. Ali Smith. *Girl Meets Boy*. New York, Canongate, 2007, pps, 89, 98.

Chapter 5

1. Leslie Marmon Silko. *Ceremony*. New York: Viking Penguin, 1977. Reprint 1986, p.95.

Chapter 6

1. Ted Hughes. "Myth and Education" in *Winter Pollen*. New York: Picador, 1994, pp.136–153.
2. Dr. Allan Hunter, *Princes, Frogs, and Ugly Sisters*. Forres, Scotland: Findhorn Press, 2010.

3. The ancient Greeks dealt with this by claiming that for the gods a day was, in fact, several thousand years long, as mortals understood time. The Hindu gods, similarly, exist in time that is conceived in the same way.

Chapter 7

1. T. S. Eliot's play is based on *Alcestis*, by the ancient Greek playwright Euripides, which adds another mythic dimension to its message.
2. Jim Hunter's memoir of his prisoner of war years is entitled *From Coastal Command to Captivity: the Memoir of a World War Two Airman*. Barnsley, UK: Pen and Sword, 2003.

Chapter 8

1. The earliest known actual burials that include grave goods are from the Skhul caves, Qafzeh, Israel, although there are earlier examples that may or may not have been deliberate burials. The Skhul hominids seem to have been an evolutionary deadend. See Stephen Oppenheimer. *Out of Eden: The Peopling of the World*. London: Robinson Publishing, 2003, and Philip Lieberman. *Uniquely Human*. Cambridge: Harvard University Press, 1991.
2. Leslie Marmon Silko, op cit., p.51.
3. Tollund man has been extensively studied. Sites include the official Danish site http://www.tullundman.dk. Bog burials have also been extensively examined. I refer the reader to R. Hutton. *The Pagan Religions of the Ancient British Isles: Their Nature and Legacy*. Oxford: Blackwell, 1993, and to D. Brothwell. *The Bog Man and the Archaeology of People*. London: British Museum Press, 1986. See also Brothwell's followup study, "Recent Research on the Lindow Bodies in the Context of Five Years of World Studies" in *Bog Bodies: New Discoveries and Perspectives*. London: British Museum Press, 1995, pp.100–103.
4. V. S. Naipaul, *India; A Wounded Civilization*. New York: HarperCollins, 1977.
5. John Cena interview by Barney Ronay: "How wrestling is taking over the movies," www.guardian.co.uk, Sept. 2, 2010.

Chapter 10

1. Chris Hedges. *War Is a Force That Gives Us Meaning*. New York: Anchor, 2003.
2. Joseph Campbell's observations on Japanese warrior training are from *Myths To Live By*. New York: Arkana Press, imprint of Penguin Books, 1993, pp.119–120.

Chapter 11

1. The research on heartbeat synchronization between mothers and children is cited by Joost Meerloo, in his chapter "The Universal Language of Rhythm" in Jack J. Leedy (Ed.). *Poetry Therapy: The Use of Poetry in the Treatment of Emotional Disorders*. Philadelphia: Lippincott, 1969, pp.52–66. In addition, see The Santa Barbara Graduate Institute movie, "What Babies Want," supporting this viewpoint. Go to www.whatbabieswant.com/synopsis.html for an outline and to order the movie. The website also quotes author Joseph Chilton-Pearce on the value of bonding immediately after birth as promoting the growth of both the child and the mother. Another similar view is to be found in Paul Pearsall, Ph.D., *The Heart's Code; Tapping the Wisdom and Power of our Heart's Energy*. New York: Broadway Books, 1998, especially pp. 66-67.

2. "The Kangaroo Care" example is cited on several news channels including http://today.msnbc.msn.com/id/38988444 (Sept. 3, 2010) and on www.nydailynews.com (Aug, 26, 2010).

3. John Chitty BCST, RPP refers to the "rescuing hug" in his online videos for the Colorado School of Energy Studies in Boulder. See: www.Youtube.com/watch?V=KE7MHnOOTc&feature+share. Other resources to back up these views are to be found in the books of Michele Odent and the lectures of Boulder midwife and nurse Karen Strange. Author Gregg Braden also refers to the rescuing hug, and featured it in his 2007 lecture series in Milan, Italy.

Chapter 14

1. Joseph Campbell. *Myths to Live By.* New York: Arkana, 1993, pp. 214–215. This material was also frequently referred to by Campbell in lectures.

2. Zozobra, whose name is Spanish for "anxiety" or "anguish," is very similar to Gormley's sculpture, since the statue is filled with notes of regret, eviction papers, divorce papers—in short, everything that Santa Fe residents want to forget about and banish. Other examples of human figures who are burned in this way include (also in New Mexico) Albuquerque's annual burning of El Kookookee (the Bogeyman), and the Holy Week celebrations of the Yaqui Indians of Mexico, who have a figure of Judas. This is an early form of scapegoating, where a human effigy has been substituted for a human being, or a goat. See Leviticus, 16, where Aaron selects a goat to carry the Israelite's sins.

3. Ted Hughes refers to Lorca and the *duende* in "Inner Music" in *Winter Pollen*. New York: Picador, 1994, p.246.

4. National Public Radio (NPR). *All Things Considered*. "Americans own Liverpool Soccer Club. Now what?" Dr. Rogan Taylor, interviewed by Philip Reeves. Broadcast on 19 Oct. 2010.

Chapter 16

1. *The Last Picture Show*, 1971, directed by Peter Bogdanovich. Available on Sony DVD, 1999.

Chapter 18

1. *Invictus*. Directed by Clint Eastwood, starring Morgan Freeman and Matt Damon. Available on Warner Home Video, 2010.

Chapter 19

1. "Russian criminal tattoos: breaking the code," article by Will Hodgkinson, in The Guardian.co.uk, 26 Oct 2010. www.guardian.co.uk/artanddesign/2010/oct/26/russian-criminal-tattoos.
2. In case this seems too extreme to believe, I'd direct the reader to *The Atlantic*, December 2010. Kenneth Brower's article on eminent scientist Freeman Dyson is entitled "The danger of cosmic genius." Dyson, one of the scientific world's most illustrious figures, believes in all the items I have listed, and more besides. It makes for frightening reading. See: www.theatlantic.com/magazine/archive/2010/12/the-danger-of-cosmic-genius/8026

Chapter 20

1. *Enchanted April*. Directed by Mike Newell. Adapted from Elizabeth Von Arnim's novel of the same name. Miramax, 1991.
2. *A Room with A View*. Directed and co-produced (with Ismail Merchant) by James Ivory. Based on the novel by E.M. Forster. The film was nominated for eight Oscars in 1986. BBC Warner, 1985.
3. *A Good Year*. Directed by Ridley Scott. Based on the book of the same name by Peter Mayle. 20th-Century Fox, 2007.

Chapter 22

1. See also Nicky Leach, in *Insight Guide: Florida* (London: Apa Publications, 2009): "On the Feast of Epiphany in January each year, the Greek Orthodox archbishop blesses local waters and tosses a crucifix into Spring Bayou. Boys aged 16 to 18 years old dive into the chilly waters to retrieve it and earn extra blessings for themselves and their families. A white dove, symbolizing the

Holy Spirit, is released to begin a *glendi*, or festival, with Greek food, music, and dance." She also reports that at the Gulf fishing port of Bayou La Batre, south of Mobile, Alabama, there is an annual blessing of the fleet in May (www.fleetblessing.org). She also says, "In New Mexico, during harvest time, agricultural communities hold masses and processions to the fields. Then, of course, there are Pueblo dances and other American Indian ceremonials that honor the seasonal agricultural cycles."

2. Bruce Chatwin. *The Songlines.* New York: Penguin, 1988.

3. The National Park Service at Rocky Mountain National Park makes some claims to sensitivity to the spiritual aspects of the landscape in their care as well as its physical aspects. This is also true for the Kaibab National Forest in Williams, Arizona, on the North Rim of the Grand Canyon. A visit to their websites, though, shows the Park Service as interested in these spiritual aspects only in the restricted sense that they were part of Native American life. The emphasis seems enthnological and historical, rather than vital.

Chapter 24

1. "Adlestrop" by Edward Thomas was first published in 1917. Since World War I, in which Thomas was later killed, was well under way at this time, his memory of a peaceful railway journey on June 23, 1914 is all the more poignant. He was killed in France on April 9, 1917.

2. "The Wait" by Rainer Maria Rilke, 1875–1926, extract translated by A. Poulin. The full text of the poem has been widely reprinted.

Chapter 26

1. Werner Herzog's interview appeared as a video and an article in *The Guardian UK,* 28 April 2011, by Jason Solomons and Jason Phipps: http://www.guardian.co.uk/film/audio/2011/apr/28/film-weekly-podcast-werner-herzog-ritzy?INTCMP=SRCH

Bhagavad Gita, The. Trans. Eknath Easwaran. Tomales, CA: Nilgiri Press, 1985.

Barthes, Roland. *Mythologies.* Trans. Annette Lavers. New York: Paladin, 1976.

Barton, Ruth Haley. *Sacred Rhythms: Arranging our Lives for Spiritual Transformation.* Downers Grove, IL: InterVarsity Press, 2006.

Bell, Catherine. *Ritual: Perspectives and Dimensions.* Oxford: Oxford University Press, 2009, reissue.

Berry, Wendell. *The Art of the Commonplace: The Agrarian Essays of Wendell Berry.* Berkeley, CA: Counterpoint Press, 2003.

Bierlein, J. F. *Parallel Myths.* New York: Ballantine Books, 1994.

Campbell, Joseph. *Myths to Live By.* New York: Penguin, 1993.

Chatwin, Bruce. *The Songlines.* New York: Penguin, 1988.

Eliot, T. S. *The Cocktail Party.* New York: Mariner Books, 1964.

_____. *The Wasteland.* Norton Critical Edition, ed. M. North. New York: Norton, 2000.

Graves, Robert. *The Greek Myths. Vols. 1 & 2. London: Folio Society, 2000.*

Hall, Edith. *Greek Tragedy: Suffering under the Sun. Oxford:* Oxford University Press, 2000.

Kraus, Chris, with **Simon Goldhill**, **Helene P. Foley**, and **Jas Elsner**, eds. *Visualizing the Tragic: Drama, Myth and Ritual in Greek Art and Literature.* New York: Oxford University Press USA, 2007.

Hedges, Chris. *War Is a Force That Gives Us Meaning.* New York: Anchor, 2003.

Hughes, Ted. *Winter Pollen: Occasional Prose.* W. Scammell ed. New York: Picador, 1994.

Monaghan, Patricia. *The Goddess Path: Myths, Invocations, and Rituals.* Woodbury, MN: Llewellyn Publications, 1999.

Naipaul, V. S. *India: A Wounded Civilization.* New York: HarperCollins, 1977.

Pullman, Philip. *The Golden Compass.* New York: Knopf Young Adult, 2006.

Rapaille, Clotaire. *The Culture Code: An Ingenious Way to Understand Why People Around the World Live and Buy as They Do.* New York: Broadway Books, 2007.

Rappaport, Roy. *Ritual and Religion in the Making of Humanity.* Boston, MA: Cambridge University Press, 1999.

Rutter-Sewell, N. J. *Guilty by Descent: Moral Inheritance and Decision Making in Greek Tragedy.* Oxford: Oxford University Press, 2000.

Segal, Robert A. *Myth: A Very Short Introduction.* New York: Oxford University Press USA, 2004.

Seligman, Adam, et al. *Ritual and Its Consequences: An Essay on the Limits of Sincerity.* Oxford: Oxford University Press, 2008.

Thomas, Edward. *The Collected Works of Edward Thomas.* BiblioLife, 2008. Order online through www.amazon.com.

Turner, Victor. *The Ritual Process: Structure and Anti Structure.* Piscataway, NJ: Aldine Transaction, 1995.

About the Author

Allan G. Hunter was born in England in 1955 and completed all his degrees at Oxford University, emerging with a doctorate in English Literature in 1983. His first book was *Joseph Conrad and the Ethics of Darwinism*. In 1986, after working at Fairleigh Dickinson University's British campus and at Peper Harow Therapeutic Community for disturbed adolescents, he moved to the US. For the past twenty years, he has been a professor of literature at Curry College in Massachusetts, and a therapist. He has produced two books specifically aimed at using writing and drawing exercises therapeutically - *The Sanity Manual* and *Life Passages*. Both books are based on his revolutionary interactive writing exercises, tried and proven in counselling sessions and classes. While working with clients in this way, he began to uncover the presence of a series of archetypes within their writings. This led to his present work with the formulation of the six archetypal stages of spiritual development.

Four years ago, he began teaching with the Blue Hills Writing Institute and he has remained with it ever since, working with students to explore the memoir and lifewriting. His own experience of this medium is reflected in *From Coastal Command to Captivity; The Memoir of a Second World War Airman*, a project on which he worked with his father up to the time of his death. It required extensive reworking to bring this memoir to completion. As in all his books, the emphasis is on the healing nature of the stories we weave for ourselves if we choose to connect to the archetypal tales of our culture.

For further information, see *http://allanhunter.net/*

Further Allan G. Hunter titles

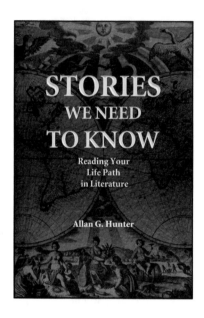

STORIES WE NEED TO KNOW

*If you're looking for reliable, time-tested guidance on your journey
through life then this is the book for you. Using the wisdom of over
three thousand years of literature and myth, Dr. Allan Hunter explores
the stories we need to know and understand, and shows how they have
offered us real advice and guidance for generations.*

978-1-84409-123-2

THE PATH OF SYNCHRONICITY

*Starting with a new explanation of synchronicity and then offering
practical instructions and exercises to tap into this collective wisdom,
the book helps readers identify the mythic patterns that guide humanity,
allowing them to face inner monsters without fear, convert them into
love and compassion, and relax as part of a universal harmony.*

978-1-84409-539-1

Further Allan G. Hunter titles

WRITE YOUR MEMOIR

Extending beyond the idea that memoir writing is intended to put past events into a more understandable current perspective, this guide maintains that keeping a document of one's life is actually the basis of a psychic process called "soul work," which manifests as a desire to experience the state of being alive to the fullest.

978-1-84409-177-5

PRINCES, FROGS & UGLY SISTERS

Discover the difference between what the Grimm brothers' tales actually say and what we think they ought to have said, and in the process find real, vital insights into how we could live more happily, understand our need for personal growth, and find our significant other.

978-1-84409-184-3

FINDHORN PRESS

Life-Changing Books

For a complete catalogue,
please contact:

Findhorn Press Ltd
117-121 High Street,
Forres IV36 1AB,
Scotland, UK

t +44 (0)1309 690582
f +44 (0)131 777 2711
e info@findhornpress.com

or consult our catalogue online
(with secure order facility) on
www.findhornpress.com

For information on the Findhorn Foundation:
www.findhorn.org